The End of Me
and My Story

A Collection of Essays on Non-Dual Teachings

JAGJOT SINGH

Disclaimer

The End of Me and My Story ("book") is intended for educational and informative purposes only and is not intended to serve as medical or professional advice.

Jagjot Singh, the author of this book is NOT a doctor, therapist, or medical health professional, nor does he give any medical advice. He is also not associated with any healthcare organization.

Nothing in this book should be viewed as a substitute for professional therapy or advice (including, without limitation, medical advice).

We assume that you take full responsibility for your physical and mental health. In case of severe health symptoms of anxiety, depression, or other psychological disorders, please consult a certified therapist or practitioner, and use information in this book only as a supplement to professional advice.

In oneself lies the whole world and if you know how to look and learn, the door is there and the key is in your hand. Nobody on earth can give you either the key or the door to open, except yourself.
Jiddu Krishnamurti

TABLE OF CONTENTS

ACKNOWLEDGMENTS

Though I print my name on this book as the author, it is not really my work but that of the Source. So, my first acknowledgment and immense gratitude go to the divinity for enabling me to channel this knowledge.

My wife, Aneesha, has been a tremendous support since the beginning of my spiritual journey. My daughter Rabani and son Rehaan fill me with joy and love through their presence and innocence.

My mother, Arvinder Singh, and my younger brother, Sartaj Singh, have been the pillars of my strength. My late father, Shri Karnail Singh, sowed the seeds of spirituality during my early years.

I sincerely thank my father-in-law, Shri Pardeep Saraf, and mother-in-law, Renu Saraf, and my brother-in-law, Karan Saraf, for providing unconditional support and love throughout my spiritual journey.

My deep gratitude to my teacher, Gautam Sachdeva, who has been a great source of strength, wisdom, and inspiration. My most profound appreciation to the masters: Jiddu Krishnamurti, Ramana Maharshi, Nisargadatta Maharaj, and Ramesh Balsekar for their great insights.

A special thanks to the editor of this book, Abha Iyengar, for all the hard work she put in editing this work.

And finally, my special thanks to all the readers who have read my articles and books and written to me over the years. Your love and support inspire me to go on.

WHAT JUST HAPPENED!

A couple of years ago, something happened. Something that I vaguely describe as "Nothingness." The reason I call it vague is that it was a non-experience experienced by nobody. For the first time, things were seen and heard without a subject or an agency experiencing them. To clarify my point, there was no "me" seeing anything, but things were seen in an impersonal sense of awareness.

Words cannot describe this non-experience, but the closest way to explain it would be something like a state of deep sleep while waking. It doesn't make sense, does it? Only when I came out of it my mind began contemplating what happened. A mere glimpse of the absence of an experiencing agency or "me", brought about a wealth of knowledge that I share with you in this book.

After this non-experience, I read the teachings of various spiritual masters like Ramana Maharshi, Nisargadatta Maharaj, Jiddu Krishnamurti, and Ramesh Balsekar, and it all made perfect sense. It deepened my understanding, and I experienced an unconditional peace of simply "being." Everything dropped. My personality dissolved, along with my identifications, beliefs, and ideologies.

There was a radical acceptance (not to be confused

with fatalism or nihilism) of the fact that the link of interconnected opposites of pleasure and pain form the basis of functioning in the duality we call life. And that while believing myself to be a separate entity with a name and form, I can do nothing to break this link of duality.

The next chapter builds the foundation for the rest of the chapters. Throughout this book, you will notice that the same message is repeated over and over again. It is not with the intention of brainwashing the readers but to enable them to verify "the message" with their own personal experience. The objective of the following essays is not to Enlighten you but to help cultivate a sense of peace and harmony in daily living by knowing one's true nature.

To explain concepts, we use an ancient Eastern teaching called *Advaita* (Non-Duality), with quotes from renowned sages of India. The concepts used in this book may seem instructional, but that's not my intention. Language makes it seem that way. We loosely refer to non-duality as a teaching, but it's neither a teaching nor a philosophy. All concepts in this book are simply pointers to the "one" unchanging absolute reality.

For the sake of simplicity, we'll continue to refer to Non-Duality as teaching because, without that setup, it is impossible to communicate and deliver concepts. Only with time and personal experience will the concepts become your living reality. And when they do, it ends the suffering — the "End of Me and My Story." The suffering dissolves along with the "me," and what remains is pure awareness or unconditional peace that is prior to thought.

THE ESSENCE OF NON-DUALITY (ADVAITA)

What follows is my interpretation of the non-dual (*Advaita*) teachings, which serves as an introduction text. It is a concept that you can explore and see if it resonates with your experiences. I do not claim to know the truth. All I'm presenting to you is a concept. What you make of it is your choice.

Advaita, for me, is not a philosophy for intellectual discussion but the pinnacle of a deep understanding one gains in this lifetime. Maybe I'm delusional or have unconscious biases, but this teaching has given me an excellent roadmap to navigate life peacefully. Please note that I'm using the word "navigate" and not "understand" life. The sense of individuality is an objectification, and the object is an appearance of a uniquely programmed entity in the dream called life. Therefore, it's impossible for this dream entity to crack the code that dictates life processes. It cannot know the basis of cosmic functioning.

Duality is not to be viewed as a philosophical or intellectual problem needing a solution. It is unsolvable because the primary and the only tool of investigation is the mind, which itself is divisive and an appearance in duality. That said, the mind is the key to non-dual understanding. While the culmination of final embodiment is the Heart, we cannot bypass the mind. The mind has to investigate and question, and through questioning, it has to realize the futility of its existence.

Understanding the essence of non-duality or teachings of Advaita is not about solving problems but dissolving them in the infinite ocean of pure consciousness — the direct experience of stillness that leaves no scope for any doubt or skepticism.

I'm not here to claim that Advaita can solve the world's burning problems like climate change, wars, violence, animal cruelty, injustice, racism, casteism, mental health challenges, etc. If you're approaching non-duality from that perspective, you'll be disappointed. If it doesn't do anything or make us better human beings, what good is it?

And the answer is, It's no good. It won't answer any questions or satisfy any of your intellectual curiosities. You cannot use it in any way for any worldly advantage. But once the pure awareness ceases the sense of individual existence all the questions dissolve. Questions arise from the fragmented mind. Pure awareness is the wholeness — the unbroken and unchanging reality that is your true essence — THAT I AM. There can be no questions in wholeness as it is complete. Sounds radical? Whether it is or not, I leave it to you, but let's explore a bit before we jump to a conclusion.

What is our primary affliction? What is the one source of all our sufferings? It is the thinking mind. Isn't it? By thinking mind, I mean the mind that is constantly concerned with the outcome or What-Should-or-Should-Not-Be rather than What-Is — the actuality of the moment. It is exhausting to live with such a mind that chooses to live anywhere except in the present or *now*.

I'm not talking about the mind that works on creative and artistic endeavors — that is the working mind, which acts spontaneously with unwavering focus on the task at hand. The working mind remains unconcerned with future outcome. The thinking, restless, or "me" mind, however, lives in time. It lives either in the dead past or an imaginary future, and hence, becomes the source of our greatest afflictions.

The thinking mind or "me" is a shape shifter. It remains obsessed with ideas and beliefs, and therefore, it is a false image created out of the past. There is no newness to the thinking mind. It thrives in time through fear and uses it to propagates suffering. It becomes belligerent when that image is exposed or threatened. While it craves freedom from the "other," what it fails to see is that its own existence is the very suffering it wants freedom from. It is the thinking mind that creates the division between "me" and the "other." This separation and the structures build around it are the root of our problems. Believing in the reality of this fictitious entity "me" and the separateness, the man frantically begins to secure it by building geographical boundaries, religions, organizations, sects, tribes, and groups with their distinct ideologies and belief systems.

This may sound complicated at the first glance, but as you go deep into the stillness, you discover that there is a substratum of all separative structures – it's the unicity or ONE energy or consciousness that is the wholeness – one without a second. It is both the source and substance of everything known and unknown.

In other words, division is a myth created by the split mind. While the "me" and the "other" appear to be separate, one cannot exist without the other. They are both simultaneously the cause and effect of each other. The "me" comes up only as a reaction to the "other," and the "other" sustains the "me". In essence, they are movements of one and the same energy.

Duality is the interplay of this energy. But that's an illusion. In reality, nothing is happening. All happening is a product of *Maya* (illusion), also known as space, time, and causation. Maya is not a separate entity but an illusion or an appearance projected by the "one" consciousness.

It is neither evil nor undesirable. Simply stated, it is phenomenality. It creates dualistic concepts such as good and evil, right and wrong, virtue and vice, moral and immoral, desirable and undesirable, so on and so forth. Therefore, every idea of happiness in life comes bundled with an almost equal, if not more, unhappiness.

Does non-dual understanding destroy the duality? No. There is nothing to destroy because it is all the same. Unicity is not apart from multiplicity. Recognition of the non-dual awareness is not the denial of multiplicity or the world that appears. A truth that changes cannot be the truth. The non-duality teaching itself is not the truth but a pointer to That which is eternal and unchanging. So, what is That unchanging which witnesses the change and is the change itself?

Introduction To the Concept

What I'm about to present is merely a concept. Every spiritual teaching is a concept. Understand the concept and verify the truth through your own life experiences. This is a difficult concept to explain but I'll do my best. My suggestion would be to go slow and take pauses to reflect every now and then.

What is the absolute truth? When we talk about truth in daily living, it is relative. It is based on something pre-existing. It doesn't stand by itself. For example, when we say that a rock is a solid substance, we assume we're talking about the abstract appearance of an object that has certain properties.

If you think in terms of quantum scale, it's difficult to know what the rock really is. It has been scientifically verified that an atom is mostly empty space. Quantum physics has shown that matter fundamentally has a wave-particle duality — it sometimes behaves as a particle and at other times behaves as a wave.

The phone that you hold in your hand — is it a wave or a particle? On the relative scale of human dimensions, it is a solid object, but on a quantum scale, it may not be that. Even your own body with the five senses is an abstraction. We can only relate to objects that are of relative scale. What is the reality then? The object that we perceive through senses or the geometrical arrangement of atoms or molecules that give it the appearance of solidity? Am I the person or subatomic particles or something else entirely?

Similar to the physical processes, the psychological abstraction creates a thinker out of a thought. Am I the thinker or the thought? Or something else entirely? This is precisely our investigation. Investigation into the nature of investigator. The nature of the observer.

My concept is that the absolute reality is unchanging and eternal. Anything that changes cannot be the absolute reality or truth. The body changes. If you doubt that, check your childhood photograph. The mind, which is a continuous flux of thoughts, feelings, and emotions, also changes. Mind is again an abstraction.

Therefore, my question to you is, what is that, that never changes? Think about it. The problem is that it's impossible to conceptualize an object that doesn't change. In fact, the unchanging truth cannot be objectified. Perception is possible only when an unchanging (relatively) subject interacts with a changing object.

For example, when we look at a flower, our unchanging gaze perceives the object (flower). The flower is changing in the sense that it is dimensionally limited in space and time. What makes the flower unique is the changing scene that the eyes perceive.

The flower is here, and it is not there. The flower moves when the wind blows. There is another flower nearby that is different in color and size. What makes the flower unique is the presence of other objects, including the background, which breaks its continuity. It makes the flower stand apart from the rest. It is what gives this flower uniqueness.

In this reality, the eyesight is the subject, and the flower is the changing object. Now, what is unchanging for the eye? The mind. The eye is simply the instrument observing the object, and the mind is superimposing attributes on it based on memory and recall.

For the eye, a flower is merely an object. The mind

tells us that it is the "flower" of so-and-so name, age, species, ugly, beautiful, and so on. Once the mind assigns attributes to the object, it is looking at the past, and entirely misses on the uniqueness of the object. In other words, what I'm looking at is my own creation brought about by thought. There is no newness to this experience. Hence, my "seeing" is incomplete. It is a filtered perception.

The eye vision changes based on different conditions and changing locations. When you get up in the morning, your vision is hazy for a short duration. What you see is based on the location of your gaze. The relatively unchanging mind "sees" the changing eyes, the changing hearing, the changing touch, and other senses. What the eyes see depends on the discriminatory capability of the mind. Therefore, the senses, in and of themselves, cannot be the truth.

What about the mind? From your own experience, you know that the mind is a flux of thoughts. Yesterday, the same flower seemed attractive. Today it's neutral. Tomorrow it may be ugly. The mind keeps changing thoughts based on changing conditions. When it's a sunny day, I'm happy. When it's cloudy, I'm depressed. The senses detect the environmental change, and the mind immediately assigns attributes based on past experiences. Therefore, the senses are changing with respect to the mind. But the mind also changes, so who is the "knower" of the changing mind?

Now it is clear that the changing mind cannot be the absolute reality. The absolute, by definition, can never change. My absolute reality cannot be different from yours. So, if you're not the changing body, or changing mind, then who are you? This question forms the basis of all spiritual seeking. Who am I? Or rather, what am I?

You are the unchanging, pure (without attributes), and eternal awareness. You are the stillness whose true nature is "knowing." You are the enabler of all perception. You are the light that illuminates the universe, but nothing illuminates you. You are self-luminous. You're both the knower and the known. You are the being-consciousness-bliss *(Sat-Chit-Ananda)*.

You are the "Isness." Your "being" cannot be different from my being. Since You make perception possible, you yourself are unknowable as an object in consciousness. You can only know objectively what you're not. But then, why do I find myself trapped in this mind-body complex and a separate world of names and forms?

You are the potential or source or oneness or God or pure consciousness that actualizes as the appearance of movement, and somehow limits itself into a mind-body complex with a finite existence, in order to experience life as we know it. The consciousness does not have an agenda other than to allow the experience. It does not function like the mind. The mind is limited, the consciousness is infinite. However, they are not two. The mind is the identified (limited) aspect of consciousness.

Therefore, one universal potential energy creates the illusion of movement as the finite minds. This movement is the contracted energy or identified consciousness or Ego that creates separation between the "me" and the "other." That is how the game of duality commences.

At the level of the absolute, there is no such thing as consciousness. The consciousness shows up as the notion of "I-thought" in the mind when it comes in contact with an object. Therefore, we say, "I am watching the object."

The "I" is a thought that comes up only when an object is experienced. The "me" is the conceptual image that rises from the identifications that the I-thought creates with the objects, ideas, concepts, beliefs, and other thoughts in linear time. Thoughts such as — I am a doctor, I am a lawyer, I am a good person, I am a bad person, I am a family person, I am an artist, I accomplished this, I failed there, — and so on. These thoughts form the personas that gives rise to the fictitious — "me and my story."

The "I-thought" or Ego creates an identification with the mind-body complex saying, "I am the body, I am the mind." However, in deep sleep (dreamless), there is no sensation of the body or mind. Hence, body and mind are not your continuous experience. Even the "me" is absent in deep sleep. But the timeless awareness — the knower of all experiences, as well as their absence, the knower of "thing" and "no-thing," is always there. It never sleeps.

You're not the thinker. You're the awareness in which thinking happens. When it goes deep, this understanding creates a natural sense of detachment from worldly pleasures and the eternal pursuit of improvement, attainment, and betterment, because you realize that you're already complete.

It breaks the illusion of separateness — "me and the others." The ego (identified consciousness) surrenders, realizing that we're only different in appearances, but the same impersonal consciousness or "I AM" runs through each mind-body organism as the aliveness. My aliveness is not different from yours. The simple understanding ends all conflicts, and hence, drops suffering.

What you really are, you cannot know as an object of experience. You are the unicity or pure awareness in which the world of names and forms appears. In fact, pure awareness is all there is — there is no flower, eyes, or mind — there's only knowing or "pure being." The Being is free from conflicts, doubts, and confusion. It is free from the question of existence or non-existence. It is neither "this" or "that." It simply "IS."

From Phenomenon to Noumenon

Many people make the mistake of thinking about non-duality as something that will make them calmer, wiser, or solve their worldly problems. Non-duality does not make any such promise. It does not solve any problems. However, the recognition of truth dissolves everything, including the one claiming to have problems. It does not answer questions but dissolves the questioner.

The ego-mind writes a script of a never-ending life drama. While the content of consciousness changes, the underlying ego-structures (I, me, mine) remain the same, causing suffering. The ego mistakes thrill and excitement for happiness and looks for fulfilment in temporary pleasures. It looks to fill a void that is none other than its own creation.

The tragedy is that there's nothing in duality that can fill this void. It keeps growing bigger with time until the mind becomes involved in an obsessive thinking pattern that it deems impossible to get out of. The primary fear is the fear of annihilation. All of the ego's actions are motivated to sustain and perpetuate the sense of separate self.

Therefore, our ego wants peace of mind in daily living, but it invariably does precisely the opposite. I've heard people say they're loving, kind, and compassionate, but their actions never match their words. There's a complete disconnect between the conscious mind and the deeper unconscious.

The ego or the limited "me" not only wants to survive but also desires to expand infinitely. It never defines limits to growth and ambition and remains in a never-ending chase for its idea of happiness.

Though the "me" asserts that it desires love and affection from others, it also enjoys drama, thrill, and anxiety associated with behavioral issues. When it cannot get what it wants, it finds covert mechanisms to seek attention by playing the victim. The root of all suffering is strong identification or grasping of the name and form as a separate entity.

In my 20s, while I struggled to make a mark in society, I often questioned my parents, "what is it that we seek by working hard and fitting in with the rest?" At one level, the answer would be money, fame, recognition, admiration, and so forth.

I would further question, "And what after that?" And they told me that all the above gave happiness and peace of mind and made us better in every aspect. But are we really happy and at peace? Do we have perfect lives? Why do we do what we do? What is it that we are really after?

Despite humanity having made so much progress in science and technology with every comfort available at the click of a button, we're experiencing severe mental health crises in the modern world. Still, there are wars and conflicts.

After many heated arguments with my parents, they

stopped the conversation by saying, "We have to do it because everyone else is doing it." And that's what it boils down to in the end. We never question anything.

Initially, it feels comfortable to not question and follow the herd blindly. It gives a false sense of security. But later, it consumes you and makes you into a hollow shell, totally disconnected from your reality.

Does it mean that we isolate ourselves in caves and disconnect ourselves from reality? No. First, you must question your concept of reality. If it changes with time, it cannot be the absolute. It is a relative reality. Question your beliefs and ideologies. Look for and see the root of your discontent and confusion.

A thousand years ago, if someone imagined life as working 9-to-5 in closed cabins, they would have been declared insane. The world of ideas and beliefs that seems real today may not be so in the times to come. In duality, change is the only constant.

Also, humans tend to see the world through the filters of minds which distorts the perception to adhere to past conditioning and pre-conceived beliefs. Although the physical world appears to be the same, each one of us interprets it differently, so how can we say it's real? The reality lies beyond the abstractions of name and form. One needs to cultivate a harmonious mind to see "that," which forms the substratum of all perceptions. As Jiddu Krishnamurti would say, see it for *what it is*.

In duality, you can have the freedom to create the life you want by freeing yourself from the grasp of the conditioned-subjugated mind, provided you challenge every belief, theory, and ideology. When you face your fears and see them totally for what they are rather than your limited perception of them through the lens of personal biases and prejudices, then only does it become possible to do so. Find out the source from where all thoughts originate. If you do that, you'll discover the truth eventually.

What does happiness mean to you? Are you chasing concepts to experience sensual pleasures by manipulating your body chemistry? Or are you seeking lasting peace that prevails, irrespective of the situations in the world?

We can attain this peace living in the world, provided we know our true nature. When the limited "me" realizes that it is unreal, our goals and ambitions fade away. I know it sounds scary because we're in love with our goals.

No material fulfillment is going to change who you are. It's not going to bring lasting peace. We have been fed this grand notion that we need to become better and worthy to gain acceptance from others, and we must prove our worth to become whole.

The bad news is that the "one" trying to achieve worthiness is never going to get it – it's never going to be satisfied with what it achieves. And the good news is that you are already whole! No destination is going to give you lasting happiness other than the *here and now*.

You're not going to discover your wholeness by my telling you what to do or not do. You must find it yourself. An approach suggested by Nisargadatta Maharaj is to 'find out what you're not,' and then you'll arrive at your natural state.

When all concepts fade, what remains is the "I AM" that shines in the bliss of pure awareness — you are That. It is a spontaneous knowing of the fact that multiplicity is an abstraction; that the same consciousness runs through each one of us, just like electricity runs through all the gadgets to carry out their designated functions.

What you perceive yourself to be, comes from memory. It is dependent on the thinking. If all your memory was gone, what would remain? What remains is the impersonal aspect of consciousness that is free from time, space, and causation. It is the constant or "being" that witnesses the mind–thoughts, feelings, emotions, sensations, and the physical world of names and forms. What is common to all life? *It is the "being."*

Please don't believe a word I say till you see the truth for yourself. Till then, question everything. Challenge every teaching and scripture–even non-duality. Non-duality is merely a concept that points to the absolute. This concept will remain untrue till you have a direct experience yourself.

Even the word absolute is a concept. You won't know the truth until you "see" (not the sight) it for yourself. Once you see it, you're out of the matrix, even while living in it. The limited "me" dissolves, and with it dissolves all concepts and beliefs that create suffering.

The outcome of this realization is unconditional peace of mind that marks the destruction of the false self ("me") or Ego, which creates suffering by strengthening the sense of separation. Let your mind wrestle with the thoughts. The understanding will happen spontaneously when the mind finally gives up and settles down. When it knows, through direct experience, that things happen, *but* there is no doer of anything.

ILLUSION AND IGNORANCE

There is a great misconception about the two words: illusion and ignorance. These words have negative connotations attached to them.

The English word ignorance implies that there is something (knowledge) lacking in "me." Therefore, I am incomplete and not whole.

If I say, "you are ignorant," you're not going to like it for sure. You'll feel offended. That is because the word ignorance is a thought in your mind associated with something you don't want to be. It triggers something, a sense of discomfort or irritation, brought about by measurement. By measurement, I mean separation between what I am and what I want or don't want to be. I'm this (wise) right now, and I don't want to be that (ignorant).

However, when the sages say that you are ignorant, their implication is entirely different. Let's understand this with the classic Vedantic example. You're walking through a dark alley and find a snake in the corner. You're in shock. The fear creates an instant reaction.

Just when you are about to run for your life, a lamppost above lights up, and you discover that what you actually thought was a snake is a piece of coiled rope. The ignorance vanishes there and then. What removed the ignorance was the instantaneous knowledge. This knowledge was not a product of the thinking mind. It was spontaneous. You did not have to think to see the snake as rope. You simply saw it for what it was.

Your mind, mistaking the rope for a snake, created the fear. For that short duration, the fear was real. Only when the light dispelled the misunderstanding, the fear was gone.

Just as the image of a snake got superimposed on the rope and produced fear, the appearance of a finite mind gets superimposed on the infinite reality. Identified with the finite, we believe the mind to be real. The mind, taking ownership of the body, believes it to be real. Therefore, in phenomenality, the mind and body become inseparable. Ignorance is believing the finite to be the only reality. Believing that I am the body, I "cling" to it. I try to prevent decay. I create desire for body's everlasting vitality and youth. And that is where my suffering begins.

Another example is when you dream, does the entity in the dream know that it is dreaming? It does not. Now, hypothetically speaking, I enter your dream and tell you that you are "ignorant" of your real nature. You may get offended in the dream, but that feeling vanishes when you wake up. It was just a dream.

All that is required for you is to wake up and see that you were dreaming. Ignorance comes from illusion which is a superimposition on reality.

It is a deliberate design of the animating consciousness. For without it, the waking dream or life as we know it would not be possible. It is required for daily interactions. I am the writer and you're the reader. While I acknowledge that's how things are in the apparent waking reality, there is an underlying awareness of that common essence which in manifestation appears as the writer and the reader of this book.

Therefore, ignorance is not something evil or undesirable. It is an attribute of the apparent reality. No relationship is possible without it. However, the undercurrent of life-force underneath is the same.

The conflict arises from the belief that appearance is the only reality. Then I desire to cling to what appears to be real in my mind. Therefore, my sense of personal existence as a separate entity in manifestation continually perpetuates the fear of non-existence.

We get offended by the word ignorance because we mistake it for a sense of lack. Our mind creates this split (measurement) of ignorance and knowledge. But they are not two separate things, because to know that you are ignorant is also knowledge. In my mind, I create an aversion to ignorance because that's how the traditional teachings have projected it as something that is undesirable, as something "you" need to get rid of in order to be wise.

Everything Happens in Consciousness

Did you come first or the universe? You may say, obviously, the universe happened first, and then I came. But notice that the universe is an appearance in your consciousness. Even the idea of time exists in your consciousness.

Your existence or non-existence is also a thought in consciousness. Being born into the world was an event in the 3D-time dimension within consciousness. Therefore, consciousness is the only reality. There cannot be a reality apart from it.

When the reality is known, the unreal does not magically disappear. The unreal is "seen" as a change, shining in the light of eternal and unchanging consciousness. The light that is self-luminous.

There is an immediate and direct shift in perception (insight). In the light of that understanding the identification with the unreal drops on its own without the person trying to "do" anything.

The idea that you did not exist before conception is usually a thought that comes from memory.

And memory is an unreliable tool. You cannot recall what you ate three days ago, so how can you know that you did not exist prior to being born.

Let's understand what is meant by illusion. The word used in the traditional texts is *Mithya* which has been loosely translated into English as the illusion. The word *Mithya* does not have an English equivalent. It means a form that is composed of lower forms.

For example, say I purchase a new car. Now the material reality of the car is that it is nothing more than an arrangement of metallic structures.

However, what makes the car valuable is the concept (the image) that I have superimposed on this gross entity. My desire creates a projection onto this metallic object whose acquisition, I believe, will make me feel enough or complete in some way.

Thus, I create an emotional attachment to the car in my mind. So, my mind superimposes images, which are psychological constructs from past knowledge. And when I believe I am the mind and emotions, it obscures the reality that is both the source and substance of the form. It is both cause and the effect.

One scratch to the car is enough to get an unpleasant reaction out of me. There's a huge difference between: "My car got scratched," and "The car got a scratch." When the object is seen for what it is, the individual can still enjoy it without creating deep attachments.

When we believe in the illusion, we create deeply unconscious attachments that come from our fears and insecurities, not from the place of love and compassion — the Heart or "Being."

Such attachments create pain not only for oneself but also for others. We become needy. Obsessive. Clingy.

What we look for in other people is a way to soothe our insecurities and not share our joyous presence with them.

In relationships, we see how people should or should not be rather than the way they are. Identification with such a limited perspective creates conflicts. When the mind is troubled, we run to psychologists, psychotherapists, and spiritual gurus for a solution.

While these things are beneficial, their effect is temporary. They do not help break down the illusion. Till the illusion sustains, the individual suffers incessantly. Believing in the illusion, we try to solve problems that are created by the illusory mind.

As I mentioned, you get to know that you were dreaming only when you wake up. In the dream, you're always convinced that it is real. Anything you consider to be the reality — ideas, beliefs, and dogmas, brings about suffering.

Clinging on to any concept or idea is bound to create suffering. Think of an idea or thought that you are firmly attached to. It may be related to your profession, religion, organization, nationalism, philosophy, or anything else.

Does it not trap you in a vicious cycle of pain and pleasure? It is mostly pain when you derive your identification from thoughts. Your thoughts are not your continuous experience. There are no thoughts in deep sleep. So how can they be the ultimate reality?

What we perceive as real is a multi-layered abstraction superimposed on one unchanging reality. The only way to break the illusion is to see the identifications for what they are.

Don't Kill the Character

In the movie of life, you don't have to kill the main character to be free from the suffering of illusion. You just have to "see" the character for what it is.

When we're watching a movie and are completely absorbed, we experience emotions and sensations. To relax, all that is required is the awareness that we're watching the movie. It comes up spontaneously. You don't have to think your way to reality. The "seeing" of reality is instantaneous.

Once "seen," the dense energy associated with the identifications becomes subtle, and that itself removes the illusion, and hence, the suffering. If the reality is so obvious, why don't we see it?

And the answer is that between reasoning and emotions, it's always the emotions that win. When the identification with underlying emotions is strong, it is impossible to see beyond them. While intellect can do wonders, it also has a dubious quality of complicating things.

It can also cause significant damage when it becomes a slave of the identifications. It makes the mind restless.

The ego does not want the truth. It wants emotional comfort or soothing of some kind that it can use or justify escaping What-Is.

Because all our life we're conditioned that way, the ego fancies the idea of arriving at the truth through personal efforts.

Deep down, we believe ourselves to be unworthy, so the idea of achievement through personal effort is appealing. The effort will only give you "what you are not," and never "what you are".

Samadhi is the cessation of all effort because in that state, there is no personal self that is pursuing an idea or goal. Therefore, what we call an illusion is a relative reality on the substratum that is pure consciousness. It is not a denial of the world (both physical and psychological). It is a recognition that what appears is relative.

A problem born out of ignorance will be solved only with a solution that comes from the same. But the solution further creates more problems. That's duality. It creates the subject-object split. Therefore, solutions born out of illusion are illusory or temporary themselves. They only appear to provide temporary satisfaction in the moment, but long-term the problems remain as before.

People seek freedom from wars, violence, corruption, malice, jealousy, hatred, and more, but they're unwilling to explore where they come from. Everything comes from within. The inner conflicts in humans manifest as wars, disease, and other evils.

The conflict is the image that is superimposed on What-Is. They remain fixated on "fixing" the outside world and making it a better place, carrying their personal idea of what is "better" or "what should be." Ramesh Balsekar calls such people the "do-gooders."

How do I know that I'm capable of knowing what's good for the world? I am not even capable of knowing what's good for me, so what makes me qualified to "do good?"

Practically every startup in Silicon Valley uses this clichéd phrase, "We aim to make the world a better place." On one hand, we, acting unconsciously, destroy nature; on the other hand, we claim to make the world a better place. We feel that we are separate from nature; that we should secure ourselves and leave nature to the creator.

There are great contradictions within us. We do exactly the opposite of what we say, and we say precisely the opposite of what we think we want. Hence, the conflict! Blindly chasing the pursuit of wealth and power, we become insensitive and unempathetic towards nature and life.

We want to be the crusaders of goodness and impose our beliefs on others without examining how these beliefs came about. We hate violence, but we're unwilling to see the violence that resides within our own shadow. I'm eager to "fix" others, but I'm reluctant to see what ails me within. It makes "me" uncomfortable. Ignorance is the blindness or unconsciousness of one's own true nature. It comes from the illusion that I am a separate entity in manifestation.

Reality of the Physical World

Hypothetically, if you see yourself at a subatomic scale, you will not find a boundary where you end and where "not you" begins. The physical limitations you typically observe at relative scales are not present at the subatomic scale. What gives shape to different body parts is the geometrical arrangement of the atoms.

Scientists have not been able to figure out what a subatomic particle is. They know what constitutes it and how it works, but they don't know what it is.

The matter composed of atoms is mostly empty space (more than 99.99999%). Some scientists recently have claimed that what we perceive as empty space has quantum fields fluctuating randomly. Quantum fields are an infinite set of harmonic oscillators.

On what basis do these oscillations happen? Why do quantum fields fluctuate and interact, and why do they impact our perception? You see, it goes on and on.

Currently, we don't have answers to such questions. We may find a scientific explanation of how things happen in the quantum world, but what its basis is, we may never know.

I may be wrong about this, but I feel that we keep finding new realities simply because we are looking. The observer produces the observed. My concept is that the consciousness produces an object based on what the subject desires. And the mind concludes, "Now I know!" But all knowing is relative.

From research in quantum mechanics, it is clear that the three states of matter (solid, liquid, and gas) we perceive typically, are abstractions, created by fluctuating quantum fields.

The fields themselves are impermanent. The perception of a subatomic particle, like an electron, happens when such fields interact to create ripples.

An electron has a lifespan of 66,000 yottayears which is quintillion times the current age of the known physical universe. The age of the particle may not be entirely accurate, but it has an end for sure (decaying into other particles). It is not something permanent. Hence, it cannot be the ultimate reality.

The reason for our suffering is not the unreal, but the belief that the unreal is the only reality. Do you know of anything that exists outside your consciousness? Consciousness is the substratum of all phenomena.

The sages say that suffering comes from the ego-mind mistaking the illusion to be the reality and the impermanent to be the permanent. That belief creates a desire to latch on to the transitory things.

The illusion, by itself, is not the problem. Spiritual awakening is waking up from the illusion, and the final deliverance is living (complete embodiment) with the awareness of reality that lies beyond the illusion.

NO TEACHING! NO METHOD! NO PRESCRIPTION!

Non-duality is not a teaching, and there's no so-called teacher that can teach you anything about it. I'm not a teacher, healer, or guru of non-duality. I'm simply a pointer.

I don't have any power or special ability that can trigger a spiritual awakening and relieve you from your sufferings. You can think of me as a spiritual reporter. Even that is not an accurate description because the one communicating with you is a persona or an image in your consciousness.

And don't get me wrong, an image or ego or sense of personal agency is required for interhuman interaction. Perhaps, that is why it exists. I'm not trying to be humble. I do admit that I have some understanding of life processes, but that does not make me either superior or inferior to anyone. It does not make me either special or ordinary in any way. As a human being experiencing life, I remain as flawed as anyone else.

Non-duality is not a philosophy or a playground for intellectual gymnastics. It is incredibly challenging to have a conversation around it because we're investigating the nature of the one making the investigation. That's why I say that I'm not a guru who has the power to awaken you. You cannot awaken until you know who YOU are.

Every Spiritual Teaching Is a Concept

Non-duality is just a concept. Every teaching or scripture is nothing but a concept. And a concept is not the Truth. But there can be no communication without concepts. Hence, concepts are used to deliver the "no-teaching" of the so-called term "non-duality."

People who say that they understand non-dual awareness are mistaken. The awareness cannot be objectified by the mind because it is the source of all perception. People mistakenly believe that an intellectual understanding of the non-dual awareness will help cure their ailments. That they can somehow use this knowledge for worldly advantages. That it can solve their financial woes; it can magically make relationships work; it can cure anxiety or depression; and so on.

We cannot use this concept as a replacement for therapy or for worldly gains or to make "our" lives better. Why? Because the very agency that strives for betterment-whatever that means-is a movement in the illusory space-time fabric. That agency is a collection of past impressions. It is a conditioned entity that is undergoing conditioning this very moment. Recognize that you are being conditioned as you read each line in this book. So, the "me" is a movement in time. Movement implies continuous change.

In duality, that we also call phenomenality, movement is a characteristic feature. We label this movement as our mind. The conditioned perception creates the illusion that we are riding on this movement (thought) or that we are the movement. When sad, I say, "I am sad." When happy, I say,

"I am happy." In other words, suffering happens when I believe that I am the thought or movement.

Think about it. If you say that you are the thought only, how do you know about it? Only the unchanging subject can know a changing object. For example, if, since your birth, the only color you had seen was red, would you know what red means?

The color red by itself does not mean anything. It derives meaning when other colors come into the picture, and the mind differentiates. We can extend the same analogy to sweet taste. The only way you know sweetness is because you have tasted saltiness. The only way you know pleasure is because you have experienced pain.

Hence, what you truly are, you can never know because there is no "other" to differentiate. You can only "know" what you're not. And so, you cannot be the mind because you're the knower of mind or movement. You are the changeless that witnesses the change. Your true nature is the eternal constant that cannot be objectified by the mind. You are the pure consciousness or stillness that is the source of all movements. You are the timeless presence. You are the self-luminous-infinite sun that never came into being nor can you be destroyed.

You are the "pure being." Once, someone asked, what is the proof that consciousness is all there is? My answer is that there is no proof other than the "being" that is your direct experience. First bring forth the entity that wants proof. The one that wants proof is a reflection in consciousness.

No teaching, method, or concept can prove consciousness because the one that's contemplating is the ego-intellect-mind. The consciousness can only be "seen" directly. It cannot be communicated to another.

The moment you try to prove consciousness, your mind has already objectified it. It has created a stripped-down version of the pure subject. The mind, being limited, applies attributes to the "attributeless". The ego-mind (mind with the reflected consciousness that identifies itself as the individual) does not like to know that it does not exist. It wants to debunk non-duality because it fears death.

That is the challenge of this concept. That is why people feel that non-duality is a radical concept. And perhaps it is. But you see, the fear of radical teaching and seeking a balanced approach to figure out the reality may itself be a radical thought.

The mind seeks comfort in familiarity and avoids uncertainty because it is uncomfortable. Therefore, the mind demands that the spiritual understanding should come in a way that seems familiar to it. The mind gives it an identification like kundalini awakening or satori or nirvana. These are mere labels.

It is the reason why different people have different ideas about spiritual awakening. It is all a part of the image that gets formed due to identifications. The conflicted mind seeks liberation but acts in a manner to strengthen the illusory image through wishes, desires, and attachments. Isn't that how we live? We desire the bliss of *nirvana*, but simultaneously, we do not want to let go of *samsara*. We maintain the division between the two with false beliefs. Who wants nirvana? And who wants to detach from samsara? That, we never question.

The Truth Cannot Be "Known" By the Illusion

No theory, ideology, belief, or dogma can tell you the Truth. The Truth comes directly into the Heart and is not a result of contemplative thinking. You cannot "think" your way to the Truth. The Truth is the unchanging subject that "you" are. Therefore, how can you know it as "an object of your experience"?

When you're awake, the waking reality is your truth. When you're asleep, it's the dreaming reality. And in deep sleep, the absence of sense objects and the mind is your truth. But who is the "knower" of waking, dreaming, and deep sleep?

The moment anyone claims to know the Truth, he or she has invented an imaginary image of the source or the ultimate reality. Any model that claims to conceptualize this Truth is not the Truth.

The models and concepts are merely the pointers. So am I. I'm not a teacher but a directionless signboard. There is no direction to "here and now." The Truth is closer to you than you think. You must arrive at the Truth through your own personal experience and understanding. It cannot be arrived at through mere words and lectures.

All I can do is give you concepts that may quench your intellectual inquisitiveness to an extent, but I'm not the agency that can bring about a spiritual understanding or insight in you.

The sense of personal agency is a concept in the mind, and as we have established above, the mind is an illusion, so how can the illusion know the Truth. Truth cannot be known as an experience. Truth is your very "being." Your essence. Your "isness." Your "nowness."

Truth cannot be discovered inside the space-time continuum because time and space imply movement. You have known time only as an inference brought about by thinking; it has no separate existence of its own. For example, if you ask, when did time come into existence, can you talk about time "outside" the time?

It's a wrong question because you're using time itself as a reference to investigate its origin, which is impossible. Concepts like "before" and "after" are relative to time. There cannot be a "when" outside time. Similarly, you may ask, what is outside space? Again, a wrong question, as there can be no "outside" when referring to space.

Time is an inference arising from the movements that give rise to events. Your existence as an individual is a function of memory propagated by the sense of time or thought.

What about space and location? When you move from point A to point B, the only reality of your location in the moment or now is point B. It is only from memory that you recall moving from point A to B. Therefore point B is reality, while point A is an inference brought about by memory.

Every point in location leading up to B is a thought that comes from the memory recall as a function of time. So, it is thinking that creates the illusion of time. In deep sleep, there is no movement, and hence, no inference of time.

Your idea of yourself being an individual with name and form as a separate entity and living a limited existence in the objective world is an illusion created by time and cannot be the Truth. The Truth is timeless.

Awakening is an impersonal spontaneous realization where the illusion of individual existence dissolves. It is not the result of a thinking mind that functions in time but the spontaneous knowing.

Suffering Comes from Identification with Movement

The main cause of our suffering is a strong identification with the movement, or what the Buddhists call "Grasping." When the pain arises, we say, "I am in pain," when the pleasure arises, we say, "I am happy."

This "I-thought" attaches itself to objects of desire (thoughts, feelings, and emotions) that manifest as a movement in time. When we're strongly bound to objects, we forget that we're the witness of the movement of objects and not the objects themselves.

The individuals who remain bound to ideas, beliefs, concepts, and dogmas suffer because they choose sides. When things happen according to our choices and preferences, we feel happy; otherwise, we remain unhappy, which is mostly the case. Choice is dualism. Choiceless awareness is non-duality.

But aren't you teaching us that we are not the body and mind? Isn't this a teaching? No, it's not. All I'm doing is telling you stories in the form of concepts. Whether it is or will become your truth depends on your personal experience. Non-duality is not a path. There's no goal. There's nothing to achieve. Life is its own goal. And what about peace of mind in daily living? This is the part that people mostly misunderstand. As the speaker or writer, I am not the least concerned about "your" (the individual) peace of mind.

We're not talking about the peace that the individual experiences due to favorable conditions. That peace can be shattered in a matter of minutes as the conditions change. I'm talking about the peace that you are, and not the one that you think you must achieve as a future goal. You already are that peace. I'm talking about the place of complete restfulness. Being itself is peace. Suffering is being this or that.

In this peace, the individual's concern with dualistic concepts of right and wrong dissolve with the recognition that there is no individual "doer" of anything. All outcomes are accepted. All feelings, thoughts, and sensations are allowed without resistance. This peace is not an outcome of an individual's effort. It is effortlessness.

It is simply the pure awareness that shines alone when the mind, realizing the futility of its efforts, suspends movement. This awareness is not an object in the mind. It is self-luminous. It is pure love. It is true freedom that the individual experiences as peace of mind with complete acceptance of What-Is.

This awareness is non-dual, and it has nothing to do with the problems of the individual experiencing the world of names and forms as a separate entity. No method or prescription can reveal this truth, nor it can completely alleviate the individual's suffering. It is the projector of illusions that forms the sense of separate existence. It is also the one that dissolves it. How? The individual cannot know as it lives within the illusion.

Methods and prescriptions may make the individual feel better temporarily. You may do meditation, yoga, therapy, cross-fit, gym, or whatever you prefer, but it only gives momentary relief. Don't get me wrong, these are incredibly beneficial, but living with the sense of individual existence, in and of itself, is like serving a rigorous imprisonment sentence.

Individual existence implies separation from the source (pure awareness), and separation is the never-ending alternating cycle of pain and pleasure. Every attempt to make the individual or person feel better is like making the prison comfortable. Do it, by all means. But a prison is a prison.

ENDING THE SUFFERING OF PERSONAL SELF

We casually throw around the word "bliss" without really understanding its true meaning. Bliss does not belong to an individual, while the suffering is always personal. It is always related to some aspect of mind and body perpetuated by past conditioning.

When something terrible happens, it happens to the individuals who think of themselves as limited entities living a finite existence in this ephemeral world. Believe it or not, all the struggle is to sustain an illusory self that is deeply absorbed in the cycle of pleasure and pain.

We like to grab pleasure and avoid pain at any cost. We live like beggars waiting for momentary happiness, here and there. But all happiness in duality is transient. Not only that, it also comes packaged with unhappiness, just like roses come with thorns.

There are fundamentally three types of actions that we perform in daily living: the first type is associated with the preservation of the biological organism, like sleeping, eating, yoga, physical exercise, meditation, work (profession), art, and more.

The second type of action is associated with social interactions, like meetings, gatherings, parties, sexual interactions, or simply sharing thoughts with another person.

The third type is creating thoughts from the sense impressions stored in memory. This action is closely related to the first two. All suffering is associated with this action because we keep ruminating about past events, which may be pleasant or unpleasant. We crave repetition of pleasant experiences and become averse to the unpleasant; both bring suffering.

We suffer recalling the past or fantasizing about the future. We replay the same stories repeatedly in our minds till they seep deep into the subconscious. The subconscious mind does not have the discriminatory capability like the conscious mind. So, it believes in whatever you feed it.

Over time, the mind becomes compulsive. At the center of all mental activity is "me," or the sense of personal identification fighting tooth and nail to survive. This "me" is a fictitious entity that arises out of ignorance.

Please understand the word ignorance. Ignorance generally has a negative connotation, but it is neither a virtue nor a vice. It is a deliberate insertion as a part of the grand design – the game of life.

Ignorance means imposing name and form on anything that appears in consciousness. Living is not possible without ignorance. For example, "human" is a concept given to a particular group of physical entities, and ignorance makes inter-human interactions possible.

Deep down, we all know that we're nothing but a collection of geometrically arranged subatomic particles. Therefore, this ignorance or abstraction is essential. The suffering happens when we become firmly attached to this abstraction (image) and believe it to be the only reality.

This abstraction is so deeply ingrained in our psyche that it's virtually impossible to imagine ourselves in any other way. All spiritual seeking is to see beyond this abstraction and realize the true self — an infinite, unchanging reality that transcends all suffering.

Buddha's first noble truth says there is suffering. For whom? It is not an absolute statement. The suffering is for the one who sees separation. Nirvana (enlightenment through cessation of desire) is when the small "I" merges with the universal "I," and the sense of separation remains only in appearances. Samsara (the world of name and form that appears from the never-ending cycle of birth, death and rebirth) is of the mind, while Nirvana is "No mind" or emptiness. Truth is the recognition that they are both one and the same. Therefore, Ramesh Balsekar emphasized that the peace of Nirvana has to be discovered while living in Samsara, as they are not two.

"Nothing of Samsara is different from Nirvana, nothing of Nirvana is different from Samsara. That which is the limit of Nirvana is also the limit of Samsara, there is not the slightest difference between the two."

Nagarjuna (Mahayana Buddhism)

Horizontal Movement of Thinking Mind

The mind can be broadly categorized into two types: The working mind — where we use critical and analytical thinking to solve problems, and the thinking mind — which sways attention in different directions, concerned with the outcome, and forms a pattern of horizontal thinking. The thinking mind is the root cause of our suffering.

When I'm writing an article, my working mind allows a space in which the words appear. It is a flow-state where I'm fully immersed in the activity and lose the sense of time. This is the creative problem-solving mind that temporarily subsides the ego. For example, when I'm engaged in an activity, I don't care about the weather or the activities happening around me. The working mind locks focus on the activity or task at hand. It only contemplates steps related to the activity, and it is not concerned with the result or outcome.

The thinking mind, on the other hand, attached to an outcome gives rise to involvement. It creates expectations and is more concerned about the result of the effort. While the working mind acts spontaneously according to the situation in the moment, the thinking mind operates in horizontal time, remaining identified with either the dead past or the imaginary future.

While performing an activity, if you find yourself bombarded with thoughts such as, "I hope people will appreciate my work," "Am I good enough," "I've always been a failure, I don't see this happening for me," and so forth – it's the thinking mind. You can see how the entire chain of the thinking mind diverts your attention from this moment or *now*.

If you're aware, you'll notice how thinking retains attention (as involvement) from one thought to another, forming a horizontal chain in time. The thinking mind suffers and creates suffering for others. It causes confusion, dissonance, indecisiveness, and hinders productivity and creativity.

The thinking mind remains preoccupied with consequences and outcomes. It is impulsive and reactive. It pins the blame on others for its failures and lives with shame and guilt. It creates pride for its successes and lives with arrogance. Whether you experience success or failure, the thinking mind perpetuates suffering by strengthening the sense of personal identification.

Even in success, it brings about doubt and skepticism

and robs you of your deserved happiness. "You did it by fluke," "You know you don't deserve this," "This is not good enough, you have to work harder," and in this way, it keeps you chasing after an imaginary satisfaction.

The result is that we keep running after more successes in the hope of something big — a greater fulfillment. We do not sit back and enjoy the fruits of our labor. We take up projects one after the other to escape the thinking mind. Yet, it is the same thinking mind that keeps us trapped on the hamster wheel.

The thinking mind strengthens itself by continually bringing attention to itself. It diverts attention from the joy of the present moment or *now*. Various ailments like anxiety and depression come from the thinking mind that is identified with the past. It invents imaginary problems based on past experiences and seeks fulfillment through temporary solutions. The solutions, created from the same consciousness as the problems, further fuel suffering.

Human ego, for personal greed of power and dominance, formed nations, by creating boundaries which gave rise to disputes, inequality, and wars. Now we humans don't want wars and violence, but are unwilling to let go of the power, dominance, and geographical boundaries. Now, to protect our boundaries, we have created nuclear weapons. That is our solution to stop the wars, but wars still happen.

Man creates divisions and then looks for solutions, to problems created by those divisions, with the divided mind. Any solution that comes from the divided mind provides temporary relief, and in the process, gives rise to new problems. The ego or the thinking mind is blind to its unconsciousness. The thinking mind is problem-oriented and operates in fear and insecurity. The real and lasting solutions to human problems will not come from thinking but from the place of deep stillness — the infinite intelligence (or the whole mind) that is beyond time.

Bliss Comes in the Silence of Stillness

Unlike the time-oriented horizontal thinking, bliss happens as an impersonal spontaneous "knowing" of the present moment or *now*. It is not the knowing of anything, but the pure knowing shining by itself. There is no individual, or subject, experiencing bliss. Simply put, it is the silence of the mind.

When the mind becomes silent, the heart spontaneously awakens, and an energy surge is felt in the body. There is no name for this state. The closest thing that can describe it is empty awareness or nothingness. It is the final abode.

A mere glimpse of this state brings about a complete transformation. It drops all suffering and questions about life and living. It is the dissolution of the ego and its sob story. It feels like waking up from a dream. In the ancient scriptures, this state is referred to as the *Turya Avastha* — the final state that is the substance and the substratum of all known states of consciousness.

In silence, there's no individual to suffer, so all that remains is pure bliss or consciousness. The mind continues in the material world, but there's no sense of personal doership. It destroys the sensitivities, heightens intuition, and gives rise to authentic creativity and genius.

But you see, the ego doesn't like the idea of its dissolution, so it keeps the mind confused by alternating between thoughts of good and evil, right and wrong, virtue and vice, and so on. For most spiritual seekers, this is the period of intense suffering, which in my understanding, is the dark night of the soul. It is a spiritual depression marked by confusion and conflict.

The mind-body organism is only an instrument through which the divine consciousness expresses itself energetically. Therefore, I don't take pride in my work as a spiritual writer, and neither do I feel fear or shame. I am also not concerned about how my writing will be perceived. Every thought comes from the Source. The biological organism is only a channel for the energy. Different biological organisms provide channeling for different kinds of energy, but all expressions are from the source or wholeness. It is only the identified mind that creates the dualistic perception of good and bad.

All the effort towards self-development or skill mastery is to enable a better channeling mechanism for the divinity to express itself. No individual grows. We mistakenly use the phrase "expand our consciousness."

It is the mind that expands in consciousness and not the consciousness itself. It cannot expand because it is infinite. Infinite cannot expand into anything. It is beyond the physical and psychological dimensions. Even the imagination is not powerful enough to understand the consciousness.

Some people like my writing. Some don't. Why should I be bothered when I know it's not my doing but the work of divinity? Whoever appreciates, I say thanks. Whoever condemns, I say to them, if the message does not resonate with you, you're free to explore other ideas and teachings, but the door of my heart remains open for all. My idea is never to argue my viewpoint. People come to this message because of the pull of the Source and not any individual. If I argue and assert, I'm interfering in God's work.

Moreover, the whole point of the message is to recognize the peace that is one's true nature, and that peace does not come with intellectual arguments and debates. The philosophers and spiritual gurus have been doing that since ages. Nobody can be convinced of the Truth by force. If that was true, there would have been no wars, violence, and suffering of any kind. The Truth can only be known in the silence of the Heart. The force divides because it is limited; the silence unites because it is unlimited.

The silence or stillness or presence drops all stories and fantasies and what remains is the pure, changeless, witnessing consciousness, or ceaseless watching. It is an unconditional surrender to the timeless and dimensionless presence.

"You cannot transcend what you do not know. To go beyond yourself, you must know yourself "

Nisargadatta Maharaj.

The Root of Suffering

The root of all suffering is the sense of personal self. The personal self is a self-image that is firmly embedded in the I-sense. It's not your fault. It is the natural progression of life that this happens. It is the result of conditioning over which you never had any control.

For example, factors like your gender, the family and culture you were born in, and so on, influence you. They shape your ideologies, your political and religious beliefs. If you carefully examine this, you'll notice that your entire personality is shaped through social and environmental conditioning, which in turn dictates your present-day choices.

None of the above factors were in your control. The organism acts and reacts based on conditioning. Therefore, the organism, in and of itself, is nothing more than a biological machine. The only thing that differentiates humans from animals is their ability to discriminate, which is significantly higher than animals. The human organism has a sharp intellect, and the ego-mind, claiming ownership over this faculty, creates suffering. The intellect does wonders when it comes to innovation and creativity in the phenomenal world, but it is a part of the *antahkarana* or the total inner instrument of the finite mind (not the whole mind).

There's no I-sense in a newborn child. If you shout, the child cries because of the body's reaction to a loud stimulus. The child experiences fear at that moment, and the body absorbs that energy (which may result in trauma in later years), but at this stage, there's no I-sense that says, "I'm scared." The newborn does not have the capacity to investigate why they were scolded. For them, it's a just a loud noise that creates a shock, and so they react spontaneously.

The child forgets and becomes happy the next moment when you lovingly caress, give kisses, or hand them a toy to play with. In other words, the only perfect sages that genuinely exist in this world are newborn children. They are authentically themselves and act spontaneously, depending on the situation. The adults wear a mask, pretending to be all smart and knowledgeable. The newborns operate with the pristine I-sense while in the adults, the I-sense expands in horizontal time as "me."

The I-sense emerges until about a year and a half when the child begins to interact and learn. The child becomes the center of attention. They quickly learn to get their needs met by crying, whining, and throwing tantrums.

However, a child's need for validation and attention is a genuine one. Therefore, the formation of the I-sense in children is necessary for them to communicate their needs. But as the transition happens into adulthood through layer upon layer of conditioning, this I-sense expands to create strong identifications with concepts, ideas, and beliefs.

Now the ego or "me" rises, giving rise to desires, along with the hope that they materialize. When something comes in between the person and the desire, then anger, hate, jealousy, and resentment arise in the mind. While the "me" appears to be separate from all of the above, it is one and the same. The "me" is anger, hate, jealousy, and so on.

Our desire to accumulate wealth, knowledge, and wisdom itself becomes an impediment in the path of liberation. Desires, in and of themselves, are not the problem, but the strong *grasping*, which indicates a strong attachment to the outcome, becomes the problem. The desires perpetuate the sense of personal identification.

When one gets blinded by desires, the rational mind shuts down. We become obsessed with external objects and start chasing them in the hope of lasting happiness. But this kind of happiness is short-lived. In fact, the moment you possess an object of your desire, half of its worth diminishes immediately, and then you set your eyes on another object. Suffering is the desire to make that which is perishable, everlasting.

The ego highly exaggerates needs and wants because that's the way it thrives. We get carried away, and by continually comparing ourselves with others, we compete with them. We want to have all that they have. We want to one-up them because it makes the "me" feel better.

Therefore, we mistake our wants as needs. We chase after them, and identified with that thinking, we see others as an obstacle to our desires. Therefore, the "other" becomes my enemy. The greatest misery of Man is that he thinks he is separate from his environment. This is unconscious living, where the false self derives its worth from possessions and accumulations.

Whatever support you gather to sustain the false image will keep breaking because the ego is never satisfied. Every time, it needs more. The objects of desire change, but the desires remain. The ego can never get what it wants because fulfillment is not its nature. Whatever satisfaction we achieve through our conquests is temporary, and the happiness is short-lived.

Extremism is the highest form of doership because there's tremendous identification with the beliefs and ideologies. This identification creates wars and suffering. I'm not hinting at a particular religion, group, or sect, but as individuals, our identifications run deep into our psyche.

Internally, we all have an extremist in hiding. It kills and tortures other people in imagination. It sticks to its stories of "this happened to me," "there's something wrong with me," and so forth. The center of focus is always the "me." It wants attention. It wants validation. And for that, it's willing to go to any extent.

Again, there is nothing wrong or right with this concept, but it is an unconscious behavior that creates suffering. Hell is nothing other than living in unconsciousness. Please don't take my words as the truth; verify this with your own experience.

In the words of Eckhart Tolle, "Ego is not good or bad. It's unconsciousness." The ego doesn't like it when it doesn't get what it wants. But the dilemma is that the ego doesn't know what it wants, so it keeps us running in circles. Unconsciousness is blindness to What-Is and identifies with What-Should-or-Should-not be.

Therefore, you'll notice that people with high self-centeredness assert aggressively as to how things should or should not be. They easily see blind spots in others but fail to see their own. They undertake social work and activism only to avoid facing their own inner darkness.

Is the I-sense (Ego) evil or undesirable? No. We require the I-sense for interactions and communications.

The way to achieve peace, or bliss is to understand the relationship between the I-sense and the world of events and objects. Simply witnessing the mind's contents with a non-judgmental and non-reactive awareness destroys their power to influence us.

The word "world" includes both the subtle (thoughts, feelings, and emotions) and gross (the world of physical objects and people).

Identifications by themselves do not cause suffering, but the grasping of them. I have two children, and I identify myself as their father, so I have to fulfill that role to the best of my capability. I'm also a husband, a brother, a son, and a friend, so I fulfill my roles accordingly.

But these are just roles; they don't define who I am. There's identification but no grasping. For example, we had to withdraw our children from school last year, citing financial problems due to the pandemic.

A close relative said that I'm not a dedicated father, or else I would have done everything (like borrowing money from someone) in my capacity to keep my children in that school.

It didn't bother me because I'm aware that the circumstances are not in anyone's control. I didn't say anything, and after a year, when the situation improved, we put them back in the same school. While the kids were at home, we (me and my wife) taught them ourselves and made sure they followed a daily routine.

There's no ill-feeling in my heart for that relative because I know that what he said came out of fear, or past conditioning. He had no control over the thought that came to him at that time. Neither am I creating any judgment for myself or my actions since even I am not in control of which thoughts come up in my consciousness at any time. We cannot choose our thoughts. They appear, play, and disappear in consciousness.

Fully knowing that I am not the thinker and that the outcome is not in my control, I simply did not react in that situation and took a decision (after carefully analyzing the situation) based on my understanding at that time. The decision was out of this understanding, and not out of fear.

A common question that I often get during meditation sessions is that thoughts rush in, and the mind becomes restless, the moment people sit for meditation. And my answer to that is to live in mindfulness, rather than limiting it to a daily practice. I'm not recommending this as a practice but do it when you recall. Watch your life. Life itself is a meditation that will bring changes.

If you can, watch yourself during challenging situations or when the mind is restless. Don't fight with the mind but see what goes on, with a non-judgmental awareness. You may fail initially. Please understand that you're uncovering years of conditioning, layer-by-layer. So, it is bound to be uncomfortable and challenging initially.

But when the mind becomes silent and the Heart awakens, one rests in blissful awareness. In that awareness, the suffering drops as the individual ego dissolves. What's left is the timeless presence or the empty awareness with no boundaries and limitations. All that remains is pure and unconditional love.

EGO: THE MASTER DECEIVER

The ego is a troubling monster. Isn't it? It spontaneously arises as anger and finds a target to hit. It wants to pinpoint and blame someone or something. After doing all the drama and experiencing emotional upheaval, it goes back into hiding. The ego is sneaky and covert, but is it pure evil? Let's explore.

The ego is unwilling to acknowledge its own existence. It survives by diverting attention to other things, people, and situations. The ego poses questions like: Why are "they" like that? Why do they behave in this or that way? Why don't they learn? Why do they purposely annoy me? It's always me versus them.

The above questions are a part of the basic diversion mechanism that the ego uses to divert attention from what's going on within. We rarely question, "Why did I react like that?" The ego finds an object and gets fixated, "This person is responsible for my unhappiness. Only if she changes will everything be okay, otherwise not."

Again, all of this is just a ploy. The problem is that the rise of the ego-identified thinking mind is so sudden that it highjacks the rational part of the brain. We experience overpowering emotions and feel the need to react to let go of the build-up stress.

And sometimes, despite our best understanding, a reaction happens. But when such behavior becomes habitual and normalized, it causes a lot of pain and suffering.

The ego rises rapidly, spews the venom, and goes back into hiding. It starts doing that frequently when the awareness is low. "How dare they treat me like that? What have I done to deserve such treatment? Why don't they change?"

The ego wants others to change, but it's unwilling to look at what lurks in the shadows deep within our psyche.

Even when the other person is sitting quietly, a dialogue continues in the ego-mind. What kind of clothes is she wearing? Look at her dressing sense. Look how much hair gel he has on his head? He looks ugly. She needs to lose some weight. And it goes on like this, changing the objects of experience, but with the same underlying structure.

It is all a diversion. The moment you start looking within, the ego-mind gets scared. So, it tells you that all this is useless. It doesn't work in practical life situations. You should do yoga instead. Or better yet, go check how many likes you got on Instagram. Or even better, why not check that viral video where Will Smith slaps a comedian at the Oscars. Diversion!

We're unwilling to look at our own behavior, but we are quick to point at the behavior of others.

Now, there are some cases where people deliberately try to provoke us, but such cases are rare. In the majority of cases, people don't do that, but our anxious mind thinks that the world is plotting against us. Therefore, it creates a barrier and uses diversion (eating, smoking, drinking, or numbing ourselves by scrolling the infinite pit of social media feeds) to avoid uncomfortable feelings. If you know yourself well, if you're aware of your inner world, it's unlikely that you'll react.

Having a reaction "in the moment" is not the problem. The problem is when the ego creates thoughts around it.

The diversion can happen in two ways. First, the grandiose way:

"I know I reacted, but he deserved it."

"He had it coming."

"Only if he hadn't said that, I would not have reacted."

"God chose me to deliver him his karma."

"I reacted because I was having a bad day, so it's not my fault."

"Do you realize how much job pressure I have? I showed them their right place. Don't they know who I am?"

"You give me stress."

Second, the victim mentality diversion:

"I am a horrible person."

"That's why I am lonely, and people don't like me."

"Only if I were a calmer person, I would have had a lot of friends."

"I react because my childhood was abusive."

"I do so much for others, but what do I get in return?"

"Back in the olden days, people were so nice."

"I was never such a horrible person, but he made me like this."

The Ego Like to Choose; The Awareness Is Choiceless

The ego loves to choose. It creates division with the ideas of good and bad, moral and immoral, virtue and vice, and so on. This division is the root of all conflicts. There's a deep-rooted belief that we're incomplete and unworthy; hence we need to accomplish "something" to be "somebody."

In this unconscious pursuit of "becoming" better than we are right now, we chase after ideologies, beliefs, and dogmas. We feel that we are changing things by "doing" something, but what essentially happens is that we end up creating more unconscious identifications. Instead of freeing ourselves from the thinking ego-mind, we get bound more.

I'm a Christian, Hindu, or Muslim; therefore, I must learn about my respective religions in order to become wise. I'm a Republican or Democrat; consequently, I must "do" something to change the political landscape. I'm an activist or a social worker; therefore, I must "do" something to make people understand how ignorant they are. These are all identifications in the mind. And they've got nothing to do with who we really are.

The emphasis is on "doing," which is governed by choice, rather than "being," which is choiceless. The choiceless awareness is freedom. I do not imply that you shouldn't take action. Identifications with beliefs are not the problem.

There's no problem in working towards an idea or a cause or a goal — but know that the outcome of our doing is not in our control. The ego wants a certain outcome based on certain choices it makes, and it likes to work with that belief, which creates suffering.

You run after gurus, life coaches, and spiritual teachers, hoping that they will help you attain peace of mind, but you get more entangled in the web of the thinking mind. This compulsive preoccupation with living in the dead past or an imaginary future is the source of all misery. The more you think about it, the more it strengthens the ego.

The problem is grasping or binding yourself to an

ideology or belief and then forcing it on others, based on your choice of outcome. That's why we see so many conflicts in interpersonal relationships. When this principle is understood, you work for the sheer joy of it and not for your preferred outcome or any external validation. This principle is the core of Karma Yoga philosophy (the selfless action).

We have turned the world into a marketplace and commodified every aspect of life and living, including relationships. "What can you offer me? I'll be with you only when you do what I like." Instead of being present for each other, we make demands and base all our relationships on that. It is bound to create suffering.

We expect perfection from others, but we're unwilling to look at ourselves. That's because working on oneself involves going deep within and facing the monster that sits there. We don't like the image we see within, and therefore, we keep chasing after solutions on the outside.

When you're present for your loved one — simply being present without any expectations, without telling them what to "do" or "not do" — it is the purest love, because the awareness is simply witnessing without getting entangled in "egoic" choices. You're not demanding an outcome. You're simply there for them.

It's Your Responsibility to Make "Me" Feel Happy

Some people are loud and abrasive. That ego seeks the longing to be heard. The problem is that it's unwilling to look at itself and what it is that it deeply fears. Instead, it wants attention, and tries to get it by creating a scene or ruckus.

It wants fulfillment but doesn't know how to get it. Some people are known for their notoriety. It's an unconscious way to live life because the ego is constantly chasing after ideas that are never going to give what it really wants.

Deep down, we desire to become spiritually complete or whole. That's where the word "holy" comes from. Not realizing that we are already what we seek to become, we chase after things and people to become whole. The need for attention and validation keeps the ego trapped in its own misery.

Rather than becoming aware and peaceful, we become restless and anxious. We build unrealistic expectations from people, and when they're not fulfilled, we create resentments. That is how conflicts happen, and relationships break, but we don't allow ourselves to sit back and look at what is going on within.

We remain obsessed with "fixing" the outer world. We take responsibility for other people's emotions but don't want to pay any attention to our own. In fact, we want other people to take responsibility for our emotional state.

"It's your job to make me feel better because I'm unwilling to take a peek inside myself." People don't say it out loud, but that's what's happening in the world. We try to control people and manipulate them, thinking it will give us happiness.

Ego Is Not Evil or Undesirable

Any reaction by itself is neither good nor bad. It is simply unconscious, and at times, we may not have control over it. The most enlightened sages and monks also react sometimes.

Even Ramana Maharshi would get angry when people pushed his triggers, but the anger never stuck to him, and he didn't create any dialogue around it. He saw it for what it was and let it go back to where it came from.

Nisargadatta Maharaj had a short temper and an intensely reactive personality, but he was not ego-sensitive, and the anger could never stick to him for a prolonged period. You could call him names, and he wouldn't react, but he would unleash fury only when he saw a division between "you and your true self."

Ramesh Balsekar used to tell a story where a long-time disciple of Nisargadatta Maharaj asked him a question, and Maharaj immediately fumed, "You have been coming here for so long, and you ask such a stupid question." The disciple replied, "What do I do, Maharaj, if God made me that way?" Maharaj's laughter was the loudest.

These sages did not divert attention. They were always immersed in their being. They fully understood that what's in a mind-body complex is not in anyone's control, and neither is there a fixed cause for anything.

Whichever thought arises in mind is from the Source or God. Therefore, no one has any control over the next thought that comes up in the mind but knowing that one is *not* the "thinker," the thought does not propagate as thinking or dialogues in horizontal time. And hence, the suffering is cut off almost immediately by witnessing the antics of the ego.

"Seeing" the ego with an undistorted perception, or witnessing awareness, cuts off the involvement almost instantly. The moment this sneaky ego is seen (by the witnessing awareness and not the individual) rearing its head, it gets exposed. That is the only way to become conscious of one's behavior.

Telling yourself not to be reactive will not work. It's like asking the thief to protect your valuables. The thief will pretend to be courteous, promising to protect the house while you go on vacation. The moment you leave, the thief clears the house.

Your ego will deceive you by convincing you that you're a calm person, but whenever a conflict arises, it will bring up the dialogues to divert attention from inner afflictions.

See the ego for what "it is" rather than looking for a solution outside. Ego is not evil or undesirable. This is because it forms the bases of inter-human interactions.

You, as a person, need the ego to operate in the world. In fact, ego forms the basis of all relationships. The problem is not the ego but the unconscious aspects of our personality that create problems.

When you react, it is the sneaky ego that comes up with its dialogues. It hides like the iceberg below the water. Only a small portion of it lies above the water, but there's a huge ice mountain underneath.

What brings peace and stability in life is cutting down the iceberg below the water level. The one at the top is required for daily functioning. And that's what I mean by the term "annihilation of the ego." Being conscious of your daily actions can bring about this awareness. However, there should be no shame or guilt for having an ego.

Ego is born out of ignorance, that is not knowing your true nature. The only way to remove this ignorance is to see it with total and complete undistorted awareness, without paying attention to any of the dialogues going on in your mind.

Having an ego does not imply that you're good or bad. The above-mentioned egoic dialogues are common. It is how the ego operates, thrives, and disrupts the peace of mind. The ego lives in fear. It operates in fear. Recognizing the fear cuts off the involvement of the ego, and then it has nothing to cling to anymore.

In a true sense, spiritual awakening is the cutting off of the involvement of "me and my story." And what remains after the dissolution of the ego is the pure impersonal presence that is our true nature.

The Ego's Idea of Detachment Is the Birthplace of The Most Dangerous Spiritual Ego

We can never truly be detached from anything in life. The nature of life is such that no matter how much effort we exert to separate ourselves from the world, we cannot ever completely cut-off our identifications with our ideologies and beliefs.

Think about it. Who's putting in the effort to be detached? It's the ego. Do you think it will let you do that? No. It's like making the arsonist in charge of the fire engines. It's a recipe for disaster. The idea of renunciation and detachment from the world in pursuit of spiritual awakening has an element of grand romanticism.

The ego says, "I'm the 'eternal-consciousness-bliss'. Therefore, I renounce the material world of pleasures and pain to attain permanent liberation from the cycle of birth and death." Who wants liberation? You see where I am going with this.

How can you renounce that which was never yours in the first place? It is the covert ego that is attempting to gain a back door entry. Earlier, when it was troubled with the material world, exhausted after trying to fill the inner void by pursuing material pleasures, it decided to detach. The ego is convinced that detachment is a tried and tested formula that never fails.

Now it wants enlightenment and liberation, but the same chase or pursuit continues, only the object has changed.

Earlier it was money, fame, adulation, and recognition. Now it's enlightenment. Notice how the ego plays subconsciously when it says, "I am not like the rest. I am the divine creation of God. This world is an illusion, and my real home awaits me." See the underlying ego structures that use the words "I," "me," and "mine." These structures form the basis of survival for the ego.

Back in my early days of exploring spiritual teachings, a formation took place inside of me that convinced me that I was different from the rest. It was the birth of my spiritual ego, which is one of the most dangerous deceptions.

After reading a few spiritual books and scriptures, I was convinced that I was the supreme consciousness or Brahman who had come to rescue the people on this planet as the next Buddha. I was the messiah, the chosen one, who would end all suffering in the world.

Have you ever fallen flat on your back? I have, and it hurts like hell. What I was reading in the scriptures and projecting myself to be was not in sync with my behavior with people around me. In my mind, I was convinced that I was a saint doing good to humanity. Oh my God, what a rascal I was. I still am, don't be fooled by my words.

When I saw the futility of chasing my own madness, I stopped reading spiritual books and took a deep dive within. I saw how acquiring knowledge enhanced my ego or the sense of personal identification, similar to people who boast of having alphabets after their names. And I was no different, except that I wanted to put alphabets before my name.

Whatever you learn about spirituality must resonate with your life experience. Don't be hasty in drawing conclusions, but at the same time, don't blindly believe anything.

There have been many incidents where the most renowned gurus fell from grace. There have been instances of abuse, extortion, and money laundering at many spiritual ashrams in India. To this day, it happens.

Why? Because of our idea that a guru is infallible. We create the distinctions between right and wrong. We're quick to place people on pedestals and throw them down afterward. It's the ego's favorite game. Ego loves involvement in the form of drama.

Once the guru is exposed, our ego wants to defame him and his teachings. At one point, you loved what your guru said. You were in awe. Now that the situation has changed, you feel hurt and want to get back somehow. You want to play the savior by debunking frauds. The ego finds some way to stay relevant. It's just another diversion mechanism to avoid "what is."

I heard one of Alan Watt's lectures where he mentions some Hebrew teaching that talks about the "element of irreducible rascality." Every man or woman is born with this element of rascality. It should not be seen as a vice or virtue. It is there, and nothing can be done about it.

It's a part of being human. It is not an undesirable trait. Rascality comes as a packaged deal when we sign up for life, making functioning possible in daily living. Rascality, by itself, is not the problem; the problem is unconsciousness.

When you put your guru or a spiritual teacher on a pedestal, who claims to have "got it all," you forget about their rascality element cause you're projecting your fantasy on them. Nothing can be done about it, except to see it for "what it is." Once seen, it becomes irrelevant.

A true sage (not the one wearing a robe) with complete understanding, is entirely in terms with his or her rascality. He lives in the moment rather than pondering on what he should be or should not be. He does not give prescriptions or methods to eliminate suffering. Instead, he points you to look inwards and find the cause of your suffering yourself.

The ego does the drama of renunciation and detachment. We leave the city and go into the mountain caves to meditate day and night to achieve something that is just an idea in the mind. Out of all the fanciful ideas, detachment is also one.

The idea of liberation is not detachment. Whatever you detach yourself from will continue to haunt you in your mind. All the grandiose ideas — of purifying oneself through ardent discipline and having perfect control over the senses — are of the ego.

The ego loves to control, and it's willing to torture the body and torment the mind to any extent to achieve what it deems desirable. The ego changes the objects of desire but retains the underlying structures to expand itself.

A monk once approached Jiddu Krishnamurti, saying he had undergone a castration operation to free himself from sexual desire. The man was in tears and was repenting at what he had done to himself. These kinds of things happen even today.

Understand the nature of your attachment rather than getting rid of it. When you have the mental clarity to see how external things influence you, you'll be able to make appropriate changes in your lifestyle to adapt to situations.

"Seeing" the ailment for what it is itself liberates, and not the idea of chasing liberation as a concept.

True liberation happens when the spiritual seeker realizes that there's nothing to be liberated. The entity that wants liberation does not exist. This understanding, in and of itself, frees one from the clutches of the ego-mind.

The solution comes in deep silence. In deep silence, the ego does not get room to play tricks; therefore, all the questions become irrelevant. The ego always remains fixated on finding answers to life problems, but the awareness conveys that there are no questions, and so, there are no answers. Silence is all there is.

THE NATURE OF NON-DUAL AWARENESS

Our life is mostly an action-reaction loop, and we remain stuck despite knowing its futility. Awareness brings wisdom — a profound knowledge of a different kind that disentangles the knots created by the compulsive thinking mind.

Awareness is pure knowing. It is noumenon, non-dual, and devoid of the subject-object relationship. It is not an object of perception but the one that makes perception possible.

It is self-luminous and all-pervasive. It is here and now. It is not something we have. It is what we truly are beyond the limitations of mind and body. Spiritual awakening is waking to this awareness or what the spiritual masters call "our real home."

It is neither here nor there. It is neither this nor that. It simply IS. It cannot be known objectively. Why? Because to know something, a relative reference point is necessary. Something can only be known in relation to something else.

For example, hot is known in relation to cold, love is known in relation to hate, good is known in relation to bad, small exists in relationship with big, joy is known in relation to suffering, and so on. None of the above things have any independent reality of their own.

Pure awareness is beyond the duality of interconnected opposites. It is the substratum of all happening or phenomenality. Even calling it "one" or "oneness" does not help because we know "one" only in relation to many. The ego-intellect-mind cannot make sense of it because it's not an object.

Therefore, to know something, we must reduce it to an object. And it is impossible to reduce awareness into an object of perception because it does not stand relative to anything else. Yet, it is right here, right now. It is in your present experience. It is the one enabling all perceptions along with the notion of an illusory individual perceiver.

The truth eludes us probably because it is so simple and obvious. Our conditioned minds are not used to simple things. We want to apply effort to arrive at an outcome because it makes the mind feel worthy of achievement. The ego-intellect-mind is not interested in seeking Truth. It is only interested in perpetuation itself by reinforcing the sense of separate identification.

Therefore, trying to use thought as an instrument to go beyond the conceptual thought— "me" — is impossible. Using "me" to uproot undesirable emotions like anger, hatred, greed, resentment, jealousy, and malice, will not help because the "me" is all those things.

This contracted energy of "me" creates an illusion of centered consciousness and is by nature jittery and restless. It cannot "do" anything about its restless nature unless it allows itself to dissolve in pure awareness.

After dissolution, what remains is the organism that is peaceful by nature and one with it. Not only is it peaceful, but it is also intuitively intelligent and sensitive. There is no owner of that organism to differentiate it from the rest of the world, and things are simply witnessed without the immediacy to change or control anything. It is complete unification devoid of the subject-object split.

Since the awareness is pristine and pure knowing, it cannot see itself as a separate object. There exists no separation for the awareness or pure subject. The illusion of separation arises in the mind as the pseudo-subject that sees itself as an object living in separation from the rest of the world.

The pseudo-subject or "me" then begins spiritual seeking in search of eternal truth, not knowing that IT IS already what it seeks. The very act of seeking the truth obscures the obvious reality that is here in this moment. All concepts of personal liberation, freedom (moksha), or enlightenment are fantasies of the ego mind. True liberation is that there is no one to be liberated.

The reality which is beyond time cannot be found in time through personal effort. But if the personal effort drops, there is the possibility that this simple truth be seen — not by the individual, but by his absence. In the absence of a pseudo-subject, there is no separation.

Time is just an inference born out of the changing frames animated by consciousness. It exists only in relation to the pseudo-subject. In deep sleep, the "me" is absent, and therefore, there's no experience of time.

In Christianity, the "doctrine of the Fall" talks about the concept of "original sin" found in the writings of St. Augustine. The idea is that Adam and Eve, who otherwise lived blissfully, defied God by falling for the temptation of eating the forbidden fruit. And henceforth, they created separation from God, giving rise to evils of the world like hatred, anger, jealousy, greed, lust, and so on.

In my interpretation, the above mythical story that signifies the event known as "the Fall," is actually the rise of the conceptual thought "me" or the sense of personal identification that creates separation from wholeness. The separation brings about the fear of death, which puts the "me" on an eternal chase for achieving permanency, not knowing that it itself is the very wholeness it seeks.

Ramesh Balsekar explains original sin as the pseudo-subject ("me") trying to usurp the subjectivity of the pure subject or awareness. It gives rise to the "I know better than you" thinking which creates relationship problems and other conflicts.

However, the Bible verse below, if understood in totality, puts an end to all conflict. Of course, it's my personal interpretation of the subject.

"I and the father are one."

John 10:30

Hypocrisy of the Ego-Mind

The mind that seeks liberation is the one that fears it the most. The world fears liberated minds. The minds that have come to a deep understanding that there is nothing to be sought or achieved in the name of spirituality or materialism; where any kind of seeking has stopped; where the dualistic notions of right and wrong, good and evil, moral and immoral have dissolved permanently.

The world fears such minds because they cannot be manipulated and controlled. And the identified self-conscious mind, living in fear of uncertainty, uses control as a mechanism to perpetuate separation. Giving up control is death for it, which is its ultimate fear. While it claims to desire wholeness, that is what it is most afraid of because it means its death.

All that the ego-mind wants to do is to create and sustain a story. It lives through "me and my story."

Therefore, it looks for ashrams and enlightened Gurus who can liberate it from pain and suffering. Jiddu Krishnamurti says, "Only when the mind is not fragmented, what you see in totality is the truth."

The non-fragmented mind is one where the notion of "me" and the "other" has entirely dissolved. It recognizes that the difference lies only in appearances; the consciousness animating all appearances in duality is the same. Such a mind "sees" its hypocritical nature and suspends doership by realizing its illusory existence.

It is an impersonal realization that does not come about through thinking. It does not happen by accepting a particular viewpoint and rejecting others; it does not happen by pretending to be neutral or indifferent to thoughts and things in phenomenality; it does not happen through knowledge, contemplation, or meditation of any kind. All those are just the stories of the thinking mind that identifies itself as "me."

It happens when non-dual awareness ceases individuality, destroying the sense of personal identification, and there's no rhyme and reason as to how, why, and when it chooses to do that.

Non-dual awareness pervades everything (and nothing), including "you," "me," and "the rest". It can't be known through the senses or mind because it is subtler than them. It is the eternal constant that makes perception possible. Yet, it is neither the perceiver nor the perceived.

NOT THE BODY, NOT THE MIND

Every spiritual inquiry begins with this question, "If I am not the mind and not the body, then what am I, and what's going on?" This fundamental existential question is the beginning of all spiritual seeking. Every question related to life and living eventually boils down to this question.

But there is another question that precedes this one. WHO WANTS TO KNOW?

The traditional Vedantic texts apparently use, "I am not the body; I am not the mind" or Neti-Neti (not-this-not-this) as affirmations to arrive at the source of pure consciousness, which is our true nature. The philosophy behind it is that we create suffering for ourselves by identifying with the limited mind-body organism.

Every identification, like gender, profession, diet choices, religious and other beliefs, etc., stems from identification with the body. These identifications give rise to the illusion of "me," which believes itself to the real, and hence, everything that the individual does is to strengthen the sense of this personal identification.

Therefore, this identification with "me" (or what is known as the ego-mind) becomes our greatest suffering because it believes itself to be the doer of all actions. It continually reinforces the idea that we are individuals living in the world of names and forms as separate entities.

Identified with the sense of separation, our actions are purely self-motivated. They become geared towards serving the ego by competing rather than creating peace and harmony through collaboration.

Individual existence is a painful one. Why? Because we know that the time is ticking and one day, the body will disintegrate. Therefore, for "me," the fear of death is the primal fear. The me-mind cannot sustain itself without the body. Our body is the gross expression of the subtle energy that appears as the mind. So, in essence, they are one and the same.

The ego-mind, identified with an outcome and taking ownership of its actions, creates pride and arrogance when it achieves the desired outcome; and creates guilt and remorse when it fails. Both of these create suffering in horizontal time as stories of individual success and failures.

You must have heard people boast of their past achievements, "I was so and so," "I had so much wealth," "My ancestors were royals," and so on. Some cling to an imaginary future, "One day, I will achieve success. Then I will be happy." In this movement between the past and the future, what gets missed is *the joy of the present moment.*

There is neither the past nor the future. They exist only in the individual as memory impressions. The future is a movement of the past only. In this moment or now, there is neither, but only the presence or "being."

Therefore, identifications, by themselves, have no independent reality outside the individual's consciousness. We don't need a mathematical formula to prove this. You can verify it right now at this moment.

Desire For Continuity

Identified with the limited mind-body organism, we desire permanency and continuity. That is why we have invented rebirth. It gives a false sense of security to the fearful mind. That there is something to look forward to after death — Hell or Heaven — both of these keep the ego-mind alive.

Religious organizations have invented hierarchies of heavens and hells to claim authority and righteousness. It is used to indoctrinate unsuspecting, gullible minds into dogmas, in order to exercise control over them. Therefore, such conditioned minds remain trapped between the desire for the heavens and aversion for the deepest hells.

Some think of creating indifference as a solution to escape the pain of attraction and aversion, but even that is a diversion of the ego-mind from the reality of the present moment. In fact, indifference can be more painful as it usually leads to emotional suppression. There must be "someone" here, to be indifferent. Do you see the paradox?

They assert that they know which actions are Heaven-worthy and which sins will lead us to Hell. The written word of the scriptures is held as the highest unquestionable authority. The gurus and priests are declared infallible. They have instructions on everything, ranging from world economic problems to how you should drink water.

Recently, we have seen the emergence of a new-age spiritual movement that talks about unconditional love and light. It talks of how you can manipulate the Universe to manifest money and happiness for yourself and how you can energetically align your chakras to serve your personal desires.

The idea behind all these movements is to liberate the individual. However, individual liberation is an oxymoron.

The individual identified with a sense of separate existence as name and form cannot be liberated. It is the nature of the mind to create divisions, which in turn, bring about conflicts.

The mind creates the idea of liberating the individual from the unending sorrows of life. So, it creates two images: one of an individual that is suffering now and wants liberation as a solution, and another future image of a perfect human being without suffering, resting in eternal bliss. And if it can't achieve liberation in this life, then there's an afterlife. And so, the chase for liberation begins.

The problem with repeating "not the mind, not the body" as an affirmation is that it still sustains the "I-thought" as "I am not". Ramana Maharshi was critical of using affirmations to negate. Earlier, identification begins as "I am mind and body," and afterwards, a new identification forms, as "I am not the mind and body."

Our minds can be very tricky. There was a householder who left his wife after they had a troubled relationship for many years. He joined a monastic order, renouncing all worldly life. Over time, people began revering him as a great sage who exemplified courage and sacrifice for the greater good of humanity.

People would queue every morning to take his blessings. At last, he proclaimed that he was now a free man in complete control of his mind and senses. One day, he received the news that his long-forgotten wife had passed away in the city. And he said, "Finally, she got what she deserved. Good riddance."

Do you see how our minds can be so delusional? He left his wife physically, but even after all that time, separated from her, he could not get rid of the poison he had for her in his mind. How can such a mind be free? All this while he held on to her, and kept doing so, even after she passed away.

Is It Possible to Free the Mind?

Is there a possibility of ending the suffering of the thinking mind? Yes, there is a possibility, but "you," the individual, is not in control of that. It will not happen by your "doing" anything, but by simply "being" the witness to what happens. I don't know of any practice, method, or technique that can dissolve the sense of personal identification.

The witnessing itself exposes the ego-mind, which surrenders after knowing its illusory nature. It "sees" things for what they are rather than how they should or should not be, independent of the filtered perception of the individual. For most of our lives, we remain preoccupied with changing the course of our lives according to our personal understanding of it.

Surrender suspends the movement of the mind and brings forth the awareness of stillness, which manifests as peace and harmony in daily living, irrespective of what's happening externally. It does not imply that we never experience pain and suffering. The thing is that its horizontal propagation in time — as suffering — is cut-short.

The objective is not to get rid of the identifications but to *witness* them in the light of a non-judgment and non-discriminating awareness, which sees them for what they are. Life as we know is impossible without identifications. Therefore, we need them for interpersonal interactions.

I am not my identifications. They are there in consciousness to allow the experience of living. I am pure consciousness. I am not concerned with what dissolves and what remains. I simply watch and allow the consciousness to bring forth the reality. Just like a mother putting her child to sleep becomes one with her, I let the consciousness put my ego-mind to sleep to become "one" with it.

When the identifications dissolve, the pleasure

experienced in the moment is fully experienced without the mind giving rise to pride, and similarly, the pain experienced in the moment is also fully experienced without giving rise to guilt. To conclude, mind and body are apparent happenings in consciousness. They have no existence outside consciousness.

The body is the consciousness experiencing itself as a dense reality, and the same consciousness experiences the mind as a subtle reality. It is the substratum behind all realities that cannot be grasped by the individual but can only be realized in its absence.

NOWHERE TO REACH; NOTHING TO ATTAIN

"Your duty is to be and not to be this or that. 'I am that I am' sums up the whole truth. The method is summed up in the words 'Be still'. What does stillness mean? It means destroy yourself. Because any form or shape is the cause for trouble. Give up the notion that 'I am so and so'. All that is required to realize the Self is to be still. What can be easier than that?"

Ramana Maharshi

In my view, the man who searches for enlightenment is no different from the man who works in his corporate job and looks forward to becoming the CEO.

That man is still better because he is not hypocritical. He is clear about what he wants, along with the fact that he's willing to do anything to get there.

Spiritual man, on the other hand, is hypocritical and full of dissonance. He searches for peace, not acknowledging the fact that it is the very search that is responsible for his misery.

He moves from one ashram to another; one guru to another; one book to another; he meditates and chants for hours; listens to bhajans (devotional songs); and attends kirtans (devotional singing), all in his vain search of finding the ultimate truth.

He idolizes his guru and puts him on a pedestal, for he believes that his infallible guru can give him something he does not have. That conditioning to seek and earn through personal effort is so strong that he's unwilling to look at what is right in front of him as here and now.

How is it any different from what happens in the material world, where we run after money, fame, recognition, admiration, and so on? A spiritual chase is no different from a material chase.

The spiritual man chasing unattainable goals finds himself impotent and unable to live in the world. First, he uses spiritual teachings as a mechanism to escape the material world.

After seeing the contractions and hypocrisy of spiritual masters he so vehemently and fiercely defended, he becomes depressed and bitter. Even after leaving the master, he cannot let go of the images they instilled in him.

He is still desperate to find the permanent bliss of enlightenment that brings an end to all his problems, worldly or otherwise. He imagines and objectifies permanency in some form.

He romanticizes the idea of using thought to liberate himself from compulsive thinking. Even after reading the highest scriptures and studying the most profound philosophies, he does not find peace. In fact, he finds himself more confused, irritated, and restless.

I'm not against any spiritual teaching or practices. All of them have benefits, but those benefits are confined only to the mind and body. No practice, method, or technique can be used to attain enlightenment or a permanent state.

Even Ramana Maharshi's self-inquiry was only for those who were too bound by their conditioning. He used it simply as a tool to create confusion so that devotees could break out of their conditioning.

Self-inquiry was never meant to be a pathway to enlightenment or any permanently blissful state. You see, the moment you genuinely search for an answer to the question, "Who am I?" things begin to fall apart.

For most of the world, the idea that this biological organism is purely a mechanical and robot-like structure programmed for action and reaction is inconceivable. The sense of self-consciousness or personal identification is powerful, and it resents the question, "Who am I?"

The mind creates a futile desire to become thoughtless and experience stillness. The stillness is conceived as having no thoughts, but isn't that a thought itself?

Stillness is not about blocking anything but simply being aware of the actuality of What-Is. Even in the traditional Vedantic systems, they reinforce the idea "I am Brahman" by repeating it as an affirmation.

Vedantic self-inquiry (not to be confused with Ramana Maharshi's self-inquiry) uses the Neti-Neti (not this, not this) or "I am not the mind, I am not the body" method to arrive at the ultimate Truth.

However, this does not help, because we are still not free of the conceptual "I-thought". There still remains an identity that believes itself to be Brahman — or not the mind and not the body.

And the moment our body goes through a crisis, the "I-thought" springs up, and expands horizontally, as the compulsive thinking mind.

Every spiritual teaching is a concept. And all concepts do is simply point to the truth, but they are not the truth themselves. All pointers to the truth are not pointers in the traditional sense.

Think of them as vectors of infinite magnitude but without direction. Therefore, all non-duality pointers point to the here and now. Here and now is the only possibility for finite to become infinite.

And that is not a state which has any worldly advantage whatsoever. It is not apart from the truth. It is not in another dimension but pervades all dimensions. It is not different for you or me. It is that which illuminates "me," "you," and "the rest of the world".

The greatest difficulty in talking about non-duality is that it can't be explained without the help of concepts. But the problem is that concepts themselves become a hurdle as we tend to lose ourselves in them.

Therefore, the message conveyed through a concept is not the truth but a pointer to the truth.

Any movement you make in any direction to attain any state is a diversion from the actuality of the present moment or now. The above statement is a concept and not the truth. Examine it and inquire for yourself.

For example, Buddha's first noble truth, "samsara is dukkha" (the world is suffering), is a concept. It is not an absolute statement. Anyone who totally understands this first truth is already there.

Some people see it as nihilistic and pessimistic, while for others, it's a great revelation. Suffering comes from the fear of the unknown. And life, by its very nature, is unpredictable.

Therefore, the ego-mind, fearing unpredictability and insecurity, pins the blame on the world. For the world to be suffering, there must be "someone" there to experience it that way. Once this concept is understood in principle, the rest of the noble truths become irrelevant.

For a child, the world is not suffering, and he (or she) does not even bother to ponder this question. Only the adults, with a garbage can of thinking running incessantly in their heads, contemplate the prospect of liberation, freedom, or the end of suffering.

Even the animals do not reflect on psychological suffering because they live instinctually and not intellectually. Their suffering is momentary and physical, which is not a concern for them. The animal eats whatever it can manage in the moment when hungry.

It does not complain about the quality or variety of food. The human mind, loaded with a sharp intellect, craves variety and change. This craving intensifies with time and makes the intellect subservient.

It includes the craving for a permanent state of mind of silence and stillness. That craving is no different than any other material craving. And denying or suppressing the craving exacerbates the problem, creating more pain and suffering.

Monks and priests have been doing this for ages without credibly verifiable results. They say, "We have what you're looking for. And we can give it to you if you do what we tell you."

Ramesh Balsekar told an exciting story about a rich man who was tired of the material world and decided to renounce everything in pursuit of spiritual seeking.

Therefore, he called his guru and told him that he didn't know what to do with his money and thought of giving it all to a charity. And the guru replied, "It's great that you're finally on the spiritual path, but for heaven's sake, don't do anything with the money till I come there."

Trying to get rid of the ego to attain supreme bliss is like a train trying to move without the engine. It's not going to happen, because it's just a fantasy. The realization of oneness can never be a personal understanding of the conditioned mind.

The oneness is not an experience but the absence of the "experiencer." There is no thinking or grasping of anything there. Those familiar with my story may have read about my experience in my house courtyard.

One day after waking up in the morning, I experienced complete unity and love with everything. Before that, I had no spiritual inclinations whatsoever.

I never asked for any experience. I had never done any meditation or *Sadhna*. I was a completely materialist person, chasing goals related solely to money and fame.

That indeed was an awakening moment, but that experience did not put me in any permanently blissful state. It was the beginning of spiritual seeking.

After that experience, I spent many years in loneliness and depression, suffering the confusion and conflict of obsessive thinking. At some point, the seeking stopped. I don't know when and why, but it ceased altogether.

Neither did I start my seeking, nor did I end it. But with the ending of seeking, the mind surrendered and became free of compulsive thinking. The thoughts still arise, but there's no involvement in thinking carried over as suffering in horizontal time.

The peace that I experience now is not free from the movement of life, which includes both pleasure and pain. Some days are peaceful, while others are painful.

There is no thinking or confusion around pain or suffering. Whatever happens, happens in the moment, and does not propagate horizontally in time.

For example, I have been suffering from debilitating lower back spasms for the last twenty years (it has become worse in the previous two years), and despite every treatment, the pain persists to this day.

I showed my back to doctors, chiropractors, physiotherapists, and yoga teachers. I also got imaging done that showed no physical abnormalities or deterioration, but still, there is no relief.

There are days when it is challenging to even get up

and walk, but there is no thinking around it. "Why me? What have I done to deserve this? Is it my past karma?" And so on. I continue my treatment and accept each day as it comes.

Similarly, when my father passed away a couple of years back, I cried and howled in grief. I miss his physical presence to this day, but there is never a question of why God took him away from me.

The body-mind organism that I knew as my father had to disintegrate, and so it did, according to the laws of nature. And so will this mind-body organism, known as Jagjot, disintegrate at some point in the future.

There is no fear of what will happen to my family (wife and two kids) after I'm gone. Life's natural flow continues for everyone. I feel much closer to my father now than when he was alive. I feel that with him gone, his essence has merged into mine.

Only humans remain preoccupied with this idea of attaining and grasping a permanent bliss of enlightenment through personal effort.

They want to make it look like they have earned it by working hard through decades of penance and sadhana. It includes the sacrifice of meditating for hours, long days of fasting, performing rituals, undergoing the torture of lifetime celibacy, eating selected foods, abstaining from all pleasures of life, suppressing natural desires, and completely renouncing the material world.

It is the ego-mind's favorite trick to achieve the desired goal of having no goals. It says, "Once I'm free from all the having and wanting, I will be in the supreme state of ultimate peace and bliss." Who wants ultimate bliss? Where does this desire for permanency come from?

If you still want to torture yourself in the pursuit of some imagined state, it's better to run after money and be the CEO. How can you renounce something that was never yours in the first place? And my question to you would be the same as what Jiddu Krishnamurti posed, "What at the end of it?"

BEING IMPRISONED IN THE REALM OF SEPARATION

There're countless articles and philosophical discussions on the idea that the body-mind organism susceptible to pain and suffering is like an imprisonment, or what someone would call — Hell.

The body is fragile, and even the slightest strike from nature can disintegrate it easily. The mind is even more delicate. It's eternally restless, running after sense-pleasures in bits and pieces, here and there.

In the early ages, humans formed religions to solve the problem of human suffering. But that didn't help, because the religious beliefs and dogmas themselves became the primary source of suffering.

The rapid advent of science in the last century created conveniences that alleviated physical suffering. The rise of new technologies in the previous two decades has made every consumable item available at the click of a button. Additionally, there have been groundbreaking breakthroughs in medicine and neuroscience — but psychological suffering continues.

In fact, with all the progress and advancements, we are

witnessing more isolation, loneliness, anxiety, depression, and a host of other ailments today. Despite having all the technological means to be connected with thousands of people, we have never felt so disconnected.

No matter how much we try to change the world to be a better place, either through religious ideas, spiritual teachings, scientific explanations, facts, philosophy, or data, we're experiencing a surge in separateness, resulting in interpersonal conflicts.

In a war between emotional impulses and reasoning, emotions win, for the most part, because ego-identified-mind creates, and enforces, the sense of separation.

Such a mind survives and thrives by embracing new ideas and beliefs, which it believes will put an end to its suffering. However, the mind can never get the liberation it desires most.

So why can't we find a solution to this problem of separateness? The answer is that we're relying on a tool designed to create and perpetuate separateness or duality — the mind. Any solution conceived by the mind to solve a problem will create a host of new issues.

Therefore, in the realm of separation, both evil and good, right and wrong, moral and immoral, happiness and unhappiness exist as interconnected opposites.

And often, non-duality is proposed and taught by some people as a solution to dualistic problems, but that's not the case.

Non-duality is not a solution to problems of duality. It is the dissolution of duality into the void or nothingness from where it arose. The human ego thinks it can solve the world's problems using the intellect, but intellect is subservient to identity.

A scientific mind may use scriptures to find answers to "that" which can't be explained, whereas a religious mind may cite scientific studies for doing the same.

The Western world believes that science alone will solve everything that ails and threatens human existence, while the Eastern world is mainly stuck with traditional teachings and scriptures.

You may assume I'm proposing a pessimistic or a nihilistic view, but that's not the case. Freedom from this realm of separation is possible right now, in this moment. The thing is that it is not the intellectual mind but the heart that needs awakening.

By heart, I don't mean that organ in your body. I'm talking about the spiritual heart, the eternal consciousness whose true nature is unconditional love.

It is impossible to awaken this heart until the mind wrestles with the idea of eliminating human suffering or knowing the highest truth through effort and struggle.

It is incapable of doing that because its very nature is to create assortments in the form of ideas, concepts, and beliefs. When given a challenge, all it does is conceive a new idea from its limited perception. Immediately afterward, the ego steps in to take ownership of that idea.

Once the ego fully grasps the idea, it seeks to convince other egos of its effectiveness. The ego creates an emotional story of perseverance and human sacrifice. That's how the collective ego is born.

But since we live in duality, there will be egos that accept this idea, and others will reject it, hence the conflict. The duality is characterized by conflicts where every thought is a force paired with an equal and opposite force.

Therefore, the concepts such as Hell, Heaven, and everything in between, are creations of the mind. Freedom is beyond concepts. It doesn't mean that we must eliminate all concepts — that would just be another concept, but "see" things for what they are rather than through the conditioned and filtered perception.

Concepts are essential for the survival of the organism.

Therefore, I'm not asking you to let go of every concept. That isn't possible. I'm offering a possibility to see things for what they are rather than how the mind thinks they should be.

For example, when you can see a flower without creating labels and concepts like name, species, beauty, fragrance, color, and so on, you discover something. You'll see your own essence in the object of experience, and that is the end of separation.

Similarly, if you can see concepts, ideas, and beliefs for what they are without applying the filters of conditioning, you see them simply for what they are. Then this whole idea of "things should be like this or that" disappears.

It is the surrender to "what is." It is the end of all suffering by the dissolution of doubts and conflicts that arise from separation. Separation is suffering. The natural outcome of "moving" (for the lack of an appropriate word) closer to our true essence is a feeling of peace or bliss unperturbed by external circumstances.

When this knowledge is absorbed in the core, it is a message that destroys every belief, including itself. The closest analogy would be the Trojan horse that contains warriors waiting to fire the pointers for spiritual awakening.

Your mind mistakenly brings the Trojan horse home thinking it's a gift, but the pointers are waiting to pierce the core of the ego so that the eternal sun of the spiritual heart is revealed. For some, this process is slow (dark night of the soul). For others, it's instantaneous.

We are not the constrained living organisms we believe ourselves to be. We are limitless and timeless. The closest thought in words to describe this feeling of freedom or liberation is unconditional love.

INTUITION: THE SACRED GIFT

"The intuitive mind is a sacred gift and the rational mind is a faithful servant. We have created a society that honors the servant and has forgotten the gift."

Albert Einstein

Intuition guides us at every step in our lives. But the problem is that the voice of intuition is far subtler than the voice of chatter in the mind. Most people have so much going on in their minds that they cannot access that instantaneous wisdom.

Overwhelmed by our thoughts, we completely ignore our intuition. Meditation may help heighten intuition and sharpen perception by reducing the mind's chatter, but that is not up to the individual but the will of the divine source.

Intuition is challenging to define because it is not a function of intellect. It is neither an effect nor does it have a cause. If it were not so, we would know the mechanism to decode it, and the source from which it appears.

Intuition is spontaneous, and it is not the product of

the thinking mind, or experience, as most people believe it to be. The wisdom of intuition is in the "being" that is beyond time and space. It appears not from the unknown but the "unknowable."

In language, we use phrases like harnessing the intuition or that my intuition serves me well. It is not your servant, nor is it there for your amusement. It is neither right nor wrong. It simply is what it is.

The message that intuition conveys comes to us as a thought, so the ego-mind immediately claims ownership. The thought is merely a channeling medium that has no wisdom of its own. True wisdom is timeless.

Another thing to note is that intuition is not always correct or accurate. The ideas like correct, right, wrong, accurate, inaccurate, etc., are of the ego. Intuition gives you the opportunity to come closer to the wholeness that is your true essence.

Therefore, when our intuition is wrong, and we must bear a loss of some kind, it is a pointer or an opportunity to investigate the truth of who we are. Instead, we judge our intuition and blame it for not being in alignment with "our" thinking.

For example, a couple of years ago, trusting my intuition, I made some choices that led me to an extremely uncomfortable situation. I ventured into a business collaboration in another country that couldn't materialize due to my differences with the investors.

All of this happened when I left my country, along with my wife and children. How could my intuition be so wrong? Everything was carefully assessed and calculated. Finally, after an unpleasant experience in a foreign country, we had to come back home.

When I look back, it was such a blessing, although it felt painful at that time. This incident helped me explore my inner world and the discomforts I was avoiding.

It opened a whole other possibility. I was upset at the time, but in retrospect, it was the best thing that happened. It was a direct calling from the Source.

People ask me how to harness the power of intuition. They're often keen on opening the third eye, not knowing it is the most painful thing for the ego-identified mind.

It is a shock for the mind, and there's no going back once the third-eye energy awakens. Such conditioned minds will hallucinate and go into a deep depression. It requires a deep understanding of oneself before one embarks on such a journey.

These people often have some agenda to use intuition for some material or personal benefit. If you're keen to open your Ajna chakra just for the thrill of it or for using intuition for some petty personal gain in duality, think again. I have seen some horrible repercussions of forcefully opening the third eye. The third eye is a spiritual concept, but it can have dire psychological repercussions if approached in a selfish manner.

The oneness or the Source is not concerned with the ego-identified mind's desires. Intuition is a higher reality that continuously sends the message of unity. It is spontaneously available, and we can easily tap into it when the mind is quiet. Let it naturally come to you.

Therefore, intuition is not personal, and it is not there to fulfill the ego's illusions. Trust in it means letting go of egoic control. As the mind becomes more silent, intuition will be more readily available.

Seeing it requires total attention to "What is," rather than viewing things through filters of prejudices and beliefs. It is a vibration that is subtler than that of the mind. Therefore, intuition's vibrational energy can easily penetrate the mind, but the opposite is not possible. Hence, you cannot figure it out or make any sense of why it does what it does.

THE END OF SPIRITUAL SEEKING

"Happiness is strange; it comes when you are not seeking it. When you are not making an effort to be happy, then unexpectedly, mysteriously, happiness is there, born of purity, of a loveliness of being."

J. Krishnamurti

I don't particularly like driving on the busy roads of New Delhi. I usually walk down to a nearby café which is quiet and a bit secluded. It's a good place where I like to work sometimes. On the way, there's a temple where I often see large gatherings attending religious sermons from high priests. It's a common sight in India.

One day I decided to eavesdrop from outside and listen to a couple of words, merely out of curiosity. It was a large gathering listening to a guru who wore orange-colored robes and spoke with utmost authority. I must admit that the man had a captivating voice and excellent oratory skills.

The guru began by asking the disciples to notice the notion of "me." Then he went on to explain how this "me" creates problems. By the way, the guru was not physically present there. He was imparting teachings through Zoom, and the video was being projected onto a large screen.

Finally, the guru concluded that part of the talk by declaring that to be free from this notion of "me," one must investigate their actions and make amends in behavior to purify the soul, doing which, the individual merges with the absolute or God.

He further went on to give steps and methods to do so. They included things like chanting, meditation, Japas, attending the meets regularly, being kind to one another, and some other rituals.

Do you see what happened here? The guru gave an idea of "becoming" something greater by "doing" something. He marked a destination and provided a map and methods to use it. "So, what's wrong with that?" you may ask. To be honest, nothing. In fact, everyone listening to him seemed happy.

But these very people will line up again every weekend for the rest of their lives, searching for a method to achieve merging or unification with God. Their search is never-ending, and they will most likely remain seekers until they realize what they're seeking is not apart from them.

The truth is here, right now, in this very moment. But the guru's authority and prescriptions have convinced these people that there is something to attain. And this petty human being must prove himself worthy to receive the lord's grace. Until thoroughly purified, the seeker remains unworthy.

The guru implies that something of higher significance will purify the soul. And that one has to go through arduous discipline and self-control to achieve it.

That is how a spiritual concept is twisted and transformed into a ritual-based religious concept that emphasizes purifying something considered unholy into what is considered "holy". This marks the beginning of the seeker's spiritual journey into finding wholeness.

This idea settles well with most seekers because achievement through labor, personal sacrifice, and discipline has an element of satisfaction for the ego. But the ego cannot be satisfied because that's how it is conditioned. Therefore, the seeking for the absolute or God goes on for eternity.

When you visualize God as a separate part of creation with special powers and privileges, you're simply projecting your own desirable attitudes onto him. God becomes an object of your fascination, and God-realization becomes a goal. You see, the guru has successfully convinced his disciples that there is a path to liberation.

When there's a destination to reach, i.e., the higher self, the lower self creates a desire to get there. And so, our imagination begins running wild, creating a fascinating story of struggle, hardships, and sacrifice to achieve that which is a privilege of a few.

All the prescriptions, methods, teachings, etc., become object-focused, or desire-focused: the desire for liberation from suffering. The idea is that I must become worthy through some means for a spiritual awakening to take place with the belief that those who are awake are special.

The guru emphasizes that one with the purified soul merges with God, implying that separation is the truth of the moment and unification with God is a worthy goal to achieve. And following that "event," the person in question becomes a perfectly flawless and enlightened being, just like the guru.

Now, I have nothing against the guru or his disciples because I see that dynamic simply as an (apparent) interplay between the same energy.

Therefore, all the methods, prescriptions, techniques, rituals, and so on are in some way comforting to the individual. But till there is "me" doing a practice to achieve or "become" something else, the suffering continues.

The thought of separation is the root of all our misery. It is an illusion that the ego propagates through "doing". Seeking ends, and awakening occurs, when the separation ends.

However, when one is highly fixated on the idea of liberation, the mind begins projecting. Awakening is not a personal event in time. It happens! And the understanding "comes about." To whom? Not to the ego, but an impersonal, vertical (spontaneous) thought or knowing.

Therefore, true awakening happens when the personal sense of existence dissolves into nothingness. The seeking ends when the contracted energy called "the seeker" dissipates. It is the end of "me and my story".

WATCHING THE MIND CEASELESSLY

Self-realization is the key to cultivating peace in daily living. It is the complete acceptance of "what is." The peace of mind in a self-realized person prevails even when the circumstances are unfavorable. This peace is not based on conditions but as a surrender to "What is."

It doesn't mean that we'll never experience pain. Pain is inevitable in phenomenality. But that pain doesn't translate into suffering as thinking in horizontal time. When surrender happens, the pain is accepted and witnessed by the impersonal aspect of consciousness, beyond space and time. It is what "living in the present" means.

The presence witnesses all the events without judgment or contemplation. I often sit alone for hours on the bank of Lake Sukhna in Chandigarh and look at the water and listen to its sound. At some point, the individual "me" fades, and the "listening" and "seeing" happen on their own.

The identified consciousness or the individual observing an event is always concerned with why things happen this way or that way, but the witnessing is impersonal. Therefore, this impersonal aspect of consciousness is not worried about an outcome but rests in pure awareness or your natural state.

What can we do to cultivate the presence to "be" in this natural state? And the answer is surprisingly simple. RELAX. Choose your preferred method and do it any way you like. Please don't create a punishing routine but grab the moments of awareness as they arise in your consciousness.

Simple deep breathing now and then works wonderfully for me. I know the advice sounds cliche, but most people can't do it. When people are given a method or practice, they get excited initially, but all that enthusiasm wears down after some time.

It's because the ego thrives on the idea of achievement and fulfillment. Therefore, let's say that I come up with a $1000 course on Achieving Enlightenment (whatever that means) in the comfort of your bedroom — it's appealing to the ego. Now it has a story to tell itself, "I struggled so hard and turned the tides in my favor."

True happiness doesn't come from "doing" but "being." Our "being" is not on a journey. It has no destination. It's not trying to expand or "become" whole.

There's nothing to do or achieve cause *you're already whole.*

The idea of self-realization through hardships and struggle is a fantasy of the mind and a mechanism for the ego to survive and perpetuate itself. The first spark of spiritual awakening feels uncomfortable or even traumatic for most people because the story of "me" and "myself" begins to fade. The ego identifications begin to loosen.

First, the ego desires liberation, works in that direction, studies scriptures, sutras, meditates relentlessly for years, and finally, declares itself to be liberated — the perfect human being without desires, flaws, afflictions, and defilements of any kind. It is the birthplace of know-it-all "guru" identification or the spiritual ego.

While the ego does all that, the witness simply witnesses this interplay. The ego or "I" can never be liberated because it doesn't exist in the first place — the notion of personal self results from the apparent energy contraction that comes about because of the brain fluids.

Our sense of individuality comes from memory impressions. Therefore, the thought that you are "so-and-so" is an identification in mind. Every aspect of our material existence comes from memory, which creates an image. It creates an identity, and through layered abstractions, we think of ourselves as separate individuals living in a world of names and forms.

It is not a question of right or wrong, desirable or undesirable, but "What is." If somehow, all your thoughts were wiped out, what would remain? The pure being. It is "watchfulness", "knowingness", or call it whatever you like. It's impossible to put it in words.

One can only rest in this natural state and "BE." It can't be proved because it's not an object separate from the subject. We can prove the existence of only that which is apart from us. You are it! The mind-body abstract is simply the interplay of apparent contracted energies; in reality, nothing is happening.

Duality is but a dream of the "one" consciousness or pure being. It is eternally pure. Sometimes it is conscious of sense objects, and other times, it "knows" the absence of objects of experience. Witnessing or unfiltered knowing is the continuous characteristic of the pure being. It's a stateless state.

It is there in all three states: waking, dreaming, and deep sleep. In deep sleep, it witnesses the absence of sense objects, but it is there. It is always effortlessly present. It is the final constant. It is the impersonal "self" that transcends the mind.

This essay may be a put-off for some people cause the sense of doership is firmly established in them because of past conditioning. Relaxation calms the mind and allows us to witness the effects of this layered conditioning. The witnessing, in and of itself, detaches us from the impact of our unconscious traits.

I leave you with the following quote from Nisargadatta Maharaj, which beautifully summarizes it.

Keep the 'I am' in the focus of awareness, remember that you are, watch yourself ceaselessly and the unconscious will flow into the conscious without any special effort on your part. Wrong desires and fears, false ideas, social inhibitions are blocking and preventing its free interplay with the conscious. Once free to mingle, the two become one and the one becomes all. The person merges into the witness, the witness into awareness, awareness into pure being, yet identity is not lost, only its limitations are lost.

Nisargadatta Maharaj

FREEDOM FROM THE TYRANNY OF THE "THINKING MIND"

Wearing the artificial mask of calmness, and pretending to be what you're not, is a tremendous effort. The moment you give up the facade and be authentic, you feel relieved because you have the freedom to be yourself.

The problem is when you want to be a certain way because you feel that's the way you should be. People aspire to have the calmness and composure of great saints like Ramana Maharshi.

But how calm a person is, depends on their past conditioning: the family that raised them, the schooling environment, the values they inherited from their environment, and the indoctrinated cultural beliefs.

If you were born in a "high conflict" home, where your parents had disagreements and arguments (very common), you'd likely have some psychological issues, like emotional dysregulation or some kind of fear. As a child, you learned some coping mechanisms to deal with pain, and these were carried into adulthood.

Now, you hate your childhood. You don't want to be like that, but you carry the same false image you created years ago. What could you have done? Were things in your control? Did you get to choose your family, friends, relatives, school, or enemies? So why is your *inner child* so scared?

You unknowingly carry a load on your head — the baggage of the past. And you call it "me and my sad story." The weight of that load pressures you, but you don't know what to do. The load is present when you're with your family, friends, and co-workers, and it even shows up in your dreams.

It doesn't matter how sorted you think your life is; the load is always present. It remains no matter how accomplished you think you are. No number of alphabets after your name will take that load off.

This load is the ego-mind that shows up as "I," "me," "my," and "mine." The "I" or "me" attaches itself to a story. The load is either of the dead past or future fantasies.

Thinking of the dead past, you may say to yourself, "Bad things happened to me. My dreams did not come true. My family doesn't care about me. My friends don't care. I have a horrible boss at work. I don't trust people anymore. Nobody recognizes my efforts and achievements. No matter how much I do for others, nobody respects me. I fail at every project I undertake."

In the other scenario, the mind dwells into a fantasy future. Here, the conversation to yourself may be, "I will be happy when I have a huge bank balance. I will be at peace when I become enlightened. I will be happy when I meet the person of my dreams. I will be satisfied when I'm out of the 9-to-5 grind. What will happen If I lose my job? What will I do if my investments tank? What about my future? What about my family's future?" You get the idea.

We keep swinging like a pendulum between the dead past and the imaginary future.

Do you see the tirade of the never-ending thinking mind? It goes on and on because it loves misery and victimhood. While it's natural to have these thoughts, the suffering begins when we get carried away in the stream of horizontal thinking, imagining the worst-case scenarios, one after the other.

The undercurrents of the obsessive thinking mind are so strong that one keeps ruminating on the same scenarios repeatedly. It produces such strong feelings and emotions that it hijacks the brain's ability to pause and reflect. It's like watching a series of horror shows on repeat.

Ego loves this kind of involvement, and that's how it enhances the personal sense of identification. We become more serious, more stressed, depressed and anxious. There can be no peace when the "I" or ego creates strong identifications, thinking:

"Things should be like this," or "Things should not be like that," or "I want this to happen," or "I don't want that to happen."

It is why most of our relationships are in mess. We expect people to be a certain way, and we base our happiness on that. Trying to change someone of their essential nature is an act of violence. The problem is that all discomforts and irritations are within us, but the ego loves to pin the blame on others.

So why does the ego do that? It does that because it identifies with the sense of separation — me versus others. The mind creates a strong veil that makes us believe we exist as separate identities.

This personal identification, or "me", keeps repeating the same stories. The ego's job is to keep reinforcing this fictitious image. The ego's nature is to expand and enhance itself by any means possible.

What to do then? What do you do when you've finished your water supply and see a mirage in the desert? You simply see the situation for what it is. No matter how parched you are, the mirage will not produce water.

Once you know the truth, your pain of thirst will never turn into suffering. You'll know that your momentary feeling has nothing to do with the reality of the situation.

When we see our thoughts, feelings, and emotions for what they are rather than how they should be, it is the dawn of witnessing. One witnesses things without creating judgments or reactions. So, when a painful thought arises in awareness, the thought is seen without distortion, i.e., without filtering it through the lens of past conditioning.

A space gets created between the observer and the observed that cuts off the involvement by not allowing the thought to propagate into further thinking. So, the ego does not get the opportunity to cling and get carried away by the thinking mind. As this understanding deepens, the ego gives up control, surrendering to "what is."

Suffering is a consequence of the ego getting involved in the content of consciousness. Your true nature is not either the ego or the mind. You are the pure consciousness or presence or space of pure awareness in which everything is an appearance. Your consciousness creates both the external and the internal world.

My final concept is that though we appear to exist separately in duality, it is the same consciousness that runs through all. The separation is an illusion created by the mind. Conflicts happen when we identify ourselves as the thinking, which in simple terms is our attachment to "me and my story."

Conflicts occur when my thinking contradicts yours. Since I am attached to my thoughts in the form of concepts, ideologies, and beliefs, anything that challenges them directly attacks the "me." But when the realization of oneness happens, dissolving the "me and my story", there's complete acceptance of "What is".

It is true freedom from suffering as the individual called "me" that suffers has disappeared. It is a choiceless awareness that is our natural state. Nothing can stop the momentary pain, but in the light of this new understanding, the pain does not translate into prolonged suffering.

Teaching "Them" A Lesson

One of the greatest follies of the thinking mind or ego is the idea of teaching the "other" a lesson with the firm conviction that they'll change.

I recall an incident when I was traveling in the hills of northern India. After driving and covering 300 km, we took a break at a roadside tea stall, which is a common sight in Indian hill stations.

A stranger standing close to us, waiting for his bus to come pick him up, was chewing some kind of tobacco concoction and throwing the empty pouches on the street.

My friend, seeing him litter the surroundings, got upset and started yelling at him.

His first words were something like, "Why the hell are you throwing garbage on the street?"

To which, the man gave my friend a smirk, then smiled, but did not pick up his mess.

My friend said, in a slightly toned-down manner, "If you don't pick this up, I'll call the police. You're breaking the law."

The man shrugged and said, "Sure, call the police."

After a couple of minutes, he got on his bus and spat the entire concoction he had been chewing, from the window onto the street, again, with a smirk on his face. He looked at us and laughed as the bus rode away. This was extremely upsetting for my friend, who continued calling him names even after he was out of sight.

When the ego talks, the ego listens. Genuine change does not come by force. Teaching "them" a lesson to change "them" by shaming, blaming, labeling, name-calling, etc., is a ploy of the ego to make itself feel superior or righteous.

The real change comes from within. It happens when the mind introspects and contemplates its actions. The reason why my friend was upset afterwards was that his "doership" did not get him the result he expected. If he had done the same thing with the realization that he was not the doer, then he would not have created any expectations, knowing that the outcome was not in his control.

FEELING OF ONENESS WITH THE UNIVERSE

The human ego is always geared towards self-fulfillment. It seeks enhancement in some form or the other. Its ultimate objective is to be something, or have something more, so that it feels a sense of one-upmanship on the other.

Before discussing oneness, let us understand that every human being is different, and uniquely programmed, based on past conditioning.

Therefore, duality, which is the appearance or manifestation, is the dream of "one". There may be similarities, but no two programmed psycho-physical organisms can be identical. Even in the case of twins, they may have similar physical traits, but their thinking, life choices, and destinies will be entirely different.

Though we use the word "oneness," there is no way to describe what it is, except that it is that which makes life possible as we know it. It is the "nothingness" or emptiness, from which the world of names and forms comes about.

To understand it, think of how a seed forms into a tree. The seed, by itself, does not contain the roots, shoots, branches, leaves, and fruits inside of it. If you cut open the seed, you won't find the tree condensed and packed into it. What the seed contains is the potential, or the genetic blueprint, for the tree. Therefore, from one seed, we get the entire tree —containing fruits and their respective seeds — that further contain exactly the same blueprint.

Where did the first seed come from? It came from the unmanifest. For the tree, the seed is the material cause, for the first seed, the unmanifest is the primal cause. But that is how it appears to our minds. The unmanifest, by itself, is the cause and effect of everything, including the Big Bang.

If you still want to conceptualize further, think of it as the unmanifest or potential that veils and projects itself as the actual (consciousness), stillness that gives rise to movement as the dreamlike waking reality, noumenon that manifests as the phenomenon, or in simple words — the one eternal awareness or unicity that projects itself as multiplicity, as the world of names and forms.

What we perceive as reality in the waking and dream states of consciousness is nothing but the dream of the unmanifest.

Oneness or pure consciousness is our true essence. We are the "one." How? Because the entire world appears in our consciousness. In deep sleep there is no world of multicity because there's no person or individual, but the one resting in its own grace and glory.

Realization of oneness, or self-realization, is not merely an intellectual understanding. If you intellectually convince yourself that there is "one", you'll be disappointed. You see, intellect is the function of the ego, and the "oneness" transcends the ego and the intellect.

It is the creator of the ego; therefore, it's not possible for the ego or any of its instruments to figure out what oneness is or how it functions.

Even in the dream, the individual's finite mind sees itself as multiple minds, shifting awareness from one object to another. You see this in your dreams, where your mind creates multiple objects of experience, and the subject keeps shifting awareness from one object to another.

You see yourself as various characters in the dream: sometimes you become a man, sometimes a woman, and some other times an animal or an unknown creature. Haven't you had this experience?

Therefore, convincing yourself of "oneness" is not going to work. If you sit in a lion's cage and say, "I'm one with the Universe, so it doesn't matter what happens," you'll be eaten alive. With human beings, you must be even more careful. Some people are always ready to eat some part of you if you're careless.

That said, your true nature is beyond the physical and the psychological. It is indestructible. It is both beginningless and endless. You're the witness of your body and mind that resides in its own bliss beyond any appearances.

However, for the mind, you're finite, and the fear of death of this limited entity creates the most suffering in the world. The idea of death is in reality the thought of separation between you and the "oneness". It brings up the notion that you have a limited time on this planet, therefore, you must do everything in your capacity to live well and leave behind your legacy.

While there's nothing wrong with living a decent life, but the ideas of wellness born out of fear create suffering for oneself and others. The thought that comes out of love is, "I must live well and help others to do the same," while the thought that originates from fear goes something like, "I must live well and accumulate as much as possible."

While the former is a conscious way of thinking that benefits the collective, the latter is a fear-driven unconsciousness thought to amass resources for oneself at the expense of others. While we cannot be perfect, we certainly can be more conscious.

Awakened human beings see separation at the level of physicality but know that it is the same impersonal energy that manifests as separate mind and body. Therefore, you'll notice awakened people to be reclusive and introverted. They don't hate or condemn people, but they do exercise caution when dealing with them.

You can understand the concept of "oneness" at an intellectual level, but the answer lies in the heart. Till the mind is overshadowing the heart, unification with the universal oneness, or yoga, is not possible. Unfortunately, this is the case with most people, as we have become so immersed in duality.

The happiness that we seek in the world of duality or phenomenality is purely conditional. When things happen according to what we like, we feel happy. And when things don't go according to our plans, we become restless and angry. It is a predicament of duality that one can't escape. Therefore, the peace or bliss that I talk about is not based on worldly conditions.

What Prevents Us from Seeing the Oneness?

We don't know what we want. We are simply chasing things that we have seen others do. We act like programmed robots that are the replicas of the earlier robots that programmed us. There is no universal idea of happiness, fulfillment, or contentment.

Each one of us has our own definition of the above concepts. We find happiness through the accumulation of either material concepts or the gaining of knowledge. Anything that is gained is just an enhancement of the fictional self.

Many people believe consciously or subconsciously that gaining knowledge by reading, and intellectually understanding spiritual scriptures, will lead them to liberation. However, it is the same ego shape-shifting and showing another side. Ego's very nature is deception.

Many Western philosophers make the mistake of using intellect to find a solution to the "hard problem of consciousness." In the former statement, there is an implicit assumption that consciousness is a "problem" that needs a solution, and that, in itself, is a mistake.

You see, intellect is a product of Maya or illusion, so how will it ever support the cause of its destruction? A great yogi once said, "Don't try to prove that the world is an illusion but cut down the illusion."

I see several Westerners trying to find proof of "oneness" or all-encompassing consciousness, and I ask them, "Who is it that wants to prove or disprove the "oneness"? Who are you trying to convince?"

It's the ego. And ego itself is the created object of the divine consciousness, so how can it ever know its creator? It's like a wave trying to the know the ocean. How can it do that? It is the ocean.

I'm by no means trying to denigrate the intellect. Intellectual understanding is the first step towards self-realization. Without the intellect, it's impossible to do any self-inquiry, but the awakening happens only when the intellect gives up and the ego dissolves.

The process of dissolution of ego is a painful one. The ego wants to hold on to whatever it can to survive. Therefore, self-realization happens when we give up the resistance.

People in the East are in a much more dire situation than in the West. At least, Westerners know how to use the intellect to arrive at a conclusion, whatever it may be. They're willing to use critical thinking to explore and widen their understanding.

The Eastern minds are fixated on the ancient tribal

beliefs and rituals, despite having a wealth of knowledge readily accessible. You see, no amount of knowledge can change cultural conditioning and influence. Only an open mind, willing to explore, has the possibility of self-realization.

The thing is that you seek a master to find a solution to your problems. A real master will never stroke your ego but challenge it. They will make you uncomfortable but in a compassionate manner. They will make you think rather than tell you what to do or not do. They will help you dissolve your identification with the thinking mind without giving you a method.

We seek gurus and make them our saviors because, on the inside, we believe ourselves to be inadequate, lacking the knowledge to attain liberation. But the ego is really not interested in liberation. It wants a prescription, a method to end all pain and suffering, which is nothing other than its own creation.

Therefore, you get swayed by flowery talk and grandiose claims by these so-called spiritual gurus. You put them on a pedestal, believing that their grace will free you from the bondage of pain. When that doesn't happen, you're quick to push them off the pedestal and move on to another guru.

One of the worst things people do to themselves is get attached to their own sob stories of victimhood. I'm not trying to demean anyone for being a victim or invalidate any traumatic experience that they underwent. Instead, what I'm saying is that if you don't release the painful feelings of the past, you'll remain stuck forever.

I know it sounds insensitive, but that's what the ego wants. Whatever you hold on to also holds you in the same manner. In the case of animals, the suffering is only physical, but humans suffer their own minds. Not only do we feel bad, but we also feel bad about feeling bad. It's a trap of the ego.

The ego knows how to keep you occupied, so it gives

you a lot of content to consume — a thousand ways to feel worse about yourself — and it ensures that the structures on which it survives, remain intact. So, the structures like, "Why did it happen to me?" "What did I do to deserve this?" "Why is God so unkind to me?" etc., etc., remain intact.

You keep blaming the world for diverting attention from the inner void (resulting from the egoic structures) formed and growing within you. You seek a prescription to treat the symptoms, but your ego is not interested in identifying the root cause of your ailment. That's why there is a never-ending pain.

Whatever the ego holds on to, it makes you believe that it is you. When you feel sad, the ego makes you believe that you are a sad person, and when you're happy, it makes you believe that you're a happy person. It keeps you flip-flopping between happiness and unhappiness.

Therefore, what you perceive as happiness is nothing but unhappiness because the moment conditions change and the object of your happiness disappears, you become unhappy. In other words, the happiness you're chasing is conditional and not in your control.

The "me" in you keeps resurfacing and complains about everything being wrong with the world. The external world that we see outside is an image of the internal world that we've created within us.

The "oneness" that you seek is not going to solve your worldly problems. Those problems are self-created; an illusion that has no concrete existence. Once you open your mind to the infinite consciousness, all your personal problems become insignificant. It's not that you become insensitive. You become life-sensitive as opposed to ego-sensitive.

According to Ramana Maharshi, the mind has three characteristics: tamas (inertia), rajas (activated), and sattva (pure and restful). Therefore, to realize the true self, one must bring the mind to sattva.

One can do it through meditation, devotion (bhakti), prayer, Japa (chanting), or through complete immersion in art. It doesn't matter what path you choose for self-realization. The idea is to lose the individual and rest in the grace of love, impersonal awareness, or "oneness", and become the witness of what happens.

Realization of "Oneness" Through Self-Inquiry

What lies between the one and the individual? It's an illusory concept that the individual is the doer of his actions. Many people struggle to understand this concept because we have a mechanism in the human body that prevents the individual from seeing its mechanistically programmed nature.

Therefore, this creates an illusion of the individual doer. Self-inquiry is the observation, contemplation, and questioning of who this "self" or "me" is, that believes itself to be the doer of its actions. It starts with an intellectual inquiry into the subtlest mind processes, and finally, the answer comes from the heart.

Even an intellectual understanding gives tremendous relief, but the message of "non-doership" must go deep within your being for the final realization.

You can truly understand who you are by understanding who or what you are not. Nisargadatta Maharaj has said that you attach "I am" or the sense of your being with body, thoughts, feelings, emotions, possessions, and more. These are misleading self-identifications that cause pain and misery.

You, the subject, experience an object; that is your thought. You see, if you were really your thoughts, you would never know what thinking is. The subject cannot know itself in any way without reducing it to an object of sense perception.

This is precisely the reason why we cannot know anything in this world. You can tell me everything about a subatomic particle: how it works, what impact it has on the atomic structure, its attributes like color, mass, rotation speed, etc., but you can never tell "what it is" in its entirety. You can't. That's because the reality that creates it is unmanifest; it's nothing but an appearance in the light of one universal consciousness.

So, the body, thoughts, feelings, emotions, and remembrance are all the objects of your experience, and you, as the subject, are the "experiencer" of these. The body and its processes are the gross objects, and your thoughts, feelings, and other psychological processes are the subtle objects of your experience. But none of these are you.

Watching your mind with a non-reactive awareness is the key to "oneness" realization. When the individual ego, which thinks itself to be the doer of all actions, disappears, the "oneness" is spontaneously realized.

In other words, the disappearing wave merges into the ocean and wakes up to discover that it IS, has always BEEN, and will always continue to BE the ocean, and not the limited individual wave it believed itself to be.

We become so identified with the thinking mind that it becomes impossible for us to rest in pure awareness. The mind keeps jumping from one thought to another — just like a monkey that eats half a fruit and jumps to another branch of the tree in search of another fruit without finishing the first one.

That's why our mind is called the monkey mind. It never wishes to stay in the present moment and keeps chasing after ideas in a never-ending search for happiness.

The whole idea of mindfulness is to teach the mind to stay in the present moment. In the present moment, there's just one thought, the "I AM," and that's where you reside to understand oneness.

Final Thoughts

Spiritual awakening cannot be forced; it happens. It's difficult for the priest or a man of knowledge to awaken because the knowledge in the form of beliefs is acquired, and knowledge, in and of itself, becomes a barrier to their awakening.

They spend their entire lives learning and interpreting scriptures and performing rituals without understanding the true meaning of the teachings. All teachings point to "oneness", and they're quite clear about it. Yet, their minds interpret them according to their own conditionings.

And in the process, these people unknowingly get too identified with their teachings, roles, and personalities. They feel the need to distinguish themselves from regular people by following a specific code of conduct like renouncing worldly life and its pleasures to be in service of God. They don't realize when God himself becomes an object of their desire. They exchange one set of identifications with another rather than loosening their grip on them.

It gives rise to one of the worst forms of ego, known as the spiritual ego. In that, the individual's views are not much different from the worldly materialistic views; instead of seeking material possessions, their ego diverts their attention towards seeking God or "an idea of God". So, they create a personal God, which is nothing more than a creation of their ego. They make a God not to help people but to serve their own interests.

It's easy to become a monk, renunciate the world, and run off to the caves for meditation, but it's extremely difficult to renunciate the mind; and that's where the true essence of the teaching lies. For teaching to be effective, one must learn to live in the material world and accept it for what it is. Merely wearing robes and growing a long beard does not make you an awakened soul.

Meditators who get attached to meditation will never be able to liberate themselves. Only when they rest in the bliss of impersonal awareness (even for a few seconds) do they awaken to their true nature and achieve "oneness" with the universe. At that point, the individual ego realizes that all actions that happen through the mind and body are not its own.

ENDING THE "DARK NIGHT OF THE SOUL"

Imagine how you would feel if you got to know that you've lived lies all your life. If you had this sudden realization that you're not what you believe yourself to be. There is a marked pain and confusion associated with this realization where one goes through a phase of depression, or spiritual crisis, known as the "dark night of the soul."

Spiritual awakening is the birthplace of real purity and unconditional love. It may not be a comfortable experience, but it is a beautiful one. Once fully awakened, our perception of ourselves and that of the world changes drastically. It marks the end of the personal self, and what remains is the impersonal pure and unchanging awareness.

Awakening is an impersonal event that begins to erode — layer-by-layer — your false views, ideologies, and beliefs, including the mask of personality that you hide behind. You feel naked, exposed, threatened, vulnerable and confused. That's because you've never seen yourself without the mask.

Not only that, but it also affects your interpersonal relationships, work, and other aspects of life. It creates a pain that nobody understands. You can't share this even with the people closest to you because they're entirely invested in materialism and other everyday affairs.

They're still living according to the conditioning of their environment. If you share your predicament with these people, they'll likely misunderstand, judge, or ridicule you. Even if they don't, they won't be of much help. You feel helpless, lonely, and depressed.

Even if you try to make people understand, they will convince you that you're suffering from a psychological ailment that needs immediate addressing. While it's okay to take help from therapy, in this case, that alone will not be of much help.

Generation after generation, humanity has only been producing programmed robots that lack a thinking mind of their own. Though we all have an analytical mind, we use our intellect to conform to our pre-existing beliefs without challenging their authenticity.

While it's impossible to change human beliefs and biases completely, one can question them and explore alternative views and ideas. But in some cases, the programming is so strong that it's not possible to think outside the box.

There's tremendous resistance to letting go of the programmed beliefs that keep us stuck either in the past or in the fantasies of the future. The reality is not in the past or future, but in this very moment, called now.

Spiritual awakening can be a painful process because you wake up to the one reality that you would otherwise have never imagined in your wildest dreams. This reality is unsettling because it is unconventional and complex for the mind to grasp.

In fact, it cannot be conceptualized and expressed in words, but the one experiencing awakening knows. It goes against the logical and rational mind, and initially, it isn't easy to understand what's transpiring.

Awakening is threatening for the ego. The ego wants to survive at all costs, but the spiritual awakening is the dissolution of the ego. Therefore, it fights back to survive. It comes up with rationalizations for what you are experiencing.

It scatters the mind and indents it with random thoughts to save the false image that you've believed yourself to be. The ego wants to hold on to thoughts, beliefs, and ideas because it can keep you running around chasing objects of your desire.

You see, spiritual awakening wakes up the individual ego from divine hypnosis, where the individuals experiencing awakening realize that they were never the illusory self they believed themselves to be. During this period, the spiritual seeker experience intense emotions and loneliness.

During awakening, identifications with the world of objects comprising names and forms begin to normalize, including subtle forms like feelings, thoughts, and emotions. The spiritual seeker at this time experiences panic because it is difficult to come to terms with the reality that what you call "me" does not exist.

And when there is no me, it is natural that the individual is not the doer of the actions. So, all your achievements, accomplishments, and trophies, including the adoration and admiration you gained, were never your actions. These actions just happened through the mind-body complex that the individual ego identifies as "me".

The ego tries to avoid pain and achieve pleasure. But what the ego is trying to seek in the name of pleasure is nothing but pain. Till the conditions remain favorable and the ego is getting what it wants, it will stay satisfied, but the moment conditions change to unfavorable, the ego will resent and try to avoid that change, and that, in turn, results in pain.

Breakdown of Religious and Other Social Identities

From a very early age, children receive programming from their immediate environment. All the concerned people like their parents, teachers, friends, relatives, and other people teach them the virtues they learned from their parents.

As a result, the child identifies with a particular group, sect, religion, or community. The child starts to follow certain ideologies and beliefs that penetrate deep into his or her psyche.

The I-thought creates identifications by permeating these thoughts and beliefs. The identifications in and of themselves are not the problem but the problem lies in the grasping of these concepts.

Your whole life, you have been taught what's right and wrong, the way you should behave, the moral and ethical standards you should follow, the kind of education and career path you should pursue for final happiness and fulfillment.

People around force you to conform to certain beliefs and follow rituals that make no logical sense. Your awakened mind questions, challenges, and rebels. You may argue, "But I was never forced and was always allowed to choose, and it is out of that choice that I formed my beliefs."

And to that, I ask, "What was the quality of your choice?" The life you have created for yourself today results from years of indoctrination and thinking that you acquired from people who were or are closest to you.

All your choices are limited to your conditioning. They were never really your choices. Your mind was restricted to a particular set of beliefs, and these have become so dominant that anything that challenges them will face resistance from your ego.

People who claim authority in religion tell you how to live your life based on their own psychological programming. These are robots emptying their trash and filling your mind with the garbage of moral and ethical living.

The problem is that these things change over time, but we are not allowed to question them even today. Teachers, parents, and society teach us to become good slaves. An unconscious mind is easy to subjugate than an awakened one.

People like you, who are asleep, are easy to control. You become needy, and they exploit your neediness. They keep you in the dark so that when the "poor you" bumps against a wall, some messiah is there to help and guide you.

It can be your parent, boss, or even a religious preacher. They teach you that the world is in darkness, humanity is suffering, and you, the child of all-mighty God, are responsible for restoring order and peace in the world.

This kind of thinking produces delusional and self-absorbed people. Look into history, and you'll see the sort of horrors humans created in the name of God and religion.

Out of the endless possibilities in existence, you're only given handpicked choices by these scared individuals who pass their irrational fears on to you. The most potent tool they use for control is the concept of sin and guilt.

They tell you that you have sinned, and you must pay penance. If you don't, you will burn in fiery Hell for eternity. You don't have a choice but to believe what they tell you.

During spiritual awakening, these old concepts begin to break down, and there is a great contradiction. This contradiction creates extremely painful dissonance.

It pulls the mind in two opposing directions: the intellect wants to arrive at the truth logically and deductively with sound reasoning. Still, the heart says that what you're seeking is already here at this very moment. You wonder, whom do I trust?

Your awakening is painful because the divine light that started shining in you is destroying these conditioned ideas and beliefs, one by one, and it's opening your mind to one absolute infinite reality that is your being or aliveness.

There Is Nothing You Can Call "Mine"

Let's talk about the idea of success and failure. Are good people always successful? Are lazy and uneducated people always failures? What I'm trying to say is that is there a link between an individual's nature and success? Or is there a universal idea of success or failure?

The ego creates its own definitions of success and failures based on past conditioning. If you were raised in a business family and part of a culture that supports consumerism, monetary success would be all that you desire.

This may not be the case had you been raised in a religious family or in certain parts of Southeast Asian countries where mediocrity and occupational stability are more desirable than the idea of business and entrepreneurship.

Success and failure are just concepts of the ego. It keeps us in the chase mode where the accumulation of material possessions measures an individual's worth. The more you have, the more you want, because the egoic structures like "I want/need this/that" and "I don't want/need this/that" persist.

The ego attempts to satisfy that which does not exist, so it tries by changing the objects of desire: food, alcohol, sex, drugs, then food again, sex again, and so on. The objects change, but the underlying ego structures remain.

The ego is characterized by haves and wants. It wants to achieve excellence, acquire wealth, have the best relationships, solve the mystery of life, the mystery of the Universe, and at the same time live a perfectly contented life according to its own subjective interpretations.

It is only this way that the ego survives: by keeping you running for more. But it can acquire nothing that you can call yours. Everything object of desire is transient and gives false satisfaction.

Sometimes, we compromise with our ego and settle

for these temporary pleasures, but life begins to slip as we age. The body starts to disintegrate, looks start to fade, memory starts malfunctioning, and the intellect that we proudly claim to be ours becomes dull.

No matter how much wealth we accumulate, no amount of it can compensate for the above losses. These things were never yours in the first place. They were given to you by the Source to facilitate inter-human interactions and relationships.

All your dreams, aspirations, and victories were not yours in the first place; they were merely the result of environmental conditioning. You held on to those concepts because they gave you a false sense of pride.

Now that you're waking up, you realize there's nothing you can call yours — not even your body and mind. That said, it doesn't mean that you become careless with your mind and body.

The mind-body complex is the vehicle through which the "Oneness" or "Source" or the "Universal Consciousness" manifests actions to express itself. Therefore, keeping your mind and body healthy is essential, but do so without getting over-obsessed with looks.

Everything that is born will die. I see a lot of resistance in people trying to make sense of this concept. We remain so invested in the outside world that we begin to lose ourselves in it throughout our lives. Only when the attention turns inwards, do we realize the impermanence of the material world. Then we open to the essence of our true being.

How Does Spiritual Pain End?

The pain of spiritual awakening ends when the understanding or awakening is complete. It happens when the ego dissolves, and the individual consciousness merges with the supreme cosmic consciousness. Therefore, the awakening is impersonal and timeless.

It is an experience of the (nondual) bliss of "oneness" with the entire existence. All concepts, ideas, theories, and beliefs collapse. Life continues as before but with heightened awareness and without deep involvement in duality.

The working mind becomes more productive, unleashing creativity from the deep trenches of the subconscious. On the other hand, the thinking mind, identified with the ego structures, collapses and surrenders to the divine will of the Supreme Consciousness.

It is a myth that spiritually awakened people don't contribute, and they remain self-absorbed in their own world. They don't have a world. They live in the timeless now or the present moment. It's just that their priorities shift from self-focused activities to the welfare of the collective, as they no longer see themselves as separate from others.

I'm aware that a lot of quackery goes on in the name of spiritual awakening. The so-called spiritually awakened gurus try and sell expensive courses to vulnerable people, with the promise to permanently end suffering.

Spiritual awakening is not the ending of suffering. It is the full unconditional acceptance of whatever life offers. When this acceptance happens, surrender happens. It alleviates the suffering, and peace of mind prevails in the most difficult circumstances.

Please note that awakening is not the destruction of the ego. If the ego is destroyed, the body-mind organism will also be destroyed.

Ego is required for inter-human interactions and daily functioning. Most people think that ego is identification with mind and body; however, it is not so, because even the most realized sage will respond when called by his name.

Therefore, human beings going through awakening or "the dark night of the soul" experience pain, loneliness, grief, and anger, but not hatred, rage, jealousy, and guilt. It's not that the latter emotions do not arise in the awakened souls, but their awareness is high enough not to get involved.

A self-realized master will feel a sensation of pleasure when people praise him for teaching, but it will not lead to pride or arrogance. And if it does, the master is yet not fully awakened.

A realized master will never give you methods, prescriptions, yantra, tantra, or mantra. They will simply direct you inwards and ask you to question the reality or self you call "me".

The realized master knows that whatever the ego seeks is for self-preservation and enhancement, not the truth. Throughout our life we seek self-enhancement without realizing that the self is false.

We try to make sense of things and phenomena that have no rational explanations. We hold onto material things, ideas, and beliefs, hoping to make ourselves better than what we are right now.

Therefore, the only way to end the spiritual pain is to

accept, in totality, all that is happening, realizing that no action is personal. Every action is the work of the Divine Consciousness or Source, that is both the object of experience, and also the subject experiencing the object.

Your ego is breathing its last, trying to hold on to bits and pieces of what you've accumulated over the years. But its dissolution is inevitable. You've not entirely woken up from the dream but are still in the process. That is why there's conflict, confusion, depression, anxiety, restlessness, pain, or whatever you want to call it.

Let it all go with total acceptance, as it is the will of the divine "oneness". Completely surrender to this moment and let the divine act through your body-mind mechanism. I conclude spiritual awakening with the following quote from Buddha, "Events happen, deeds are done, but there is no individual doer, thereof."

WITNESS CONSCIOUSNESS

Witnessing is the subtlest aspect of consciousness that marks the arising of a new mind or the whole mind. Nisargadatta Maharaj said that the witness is the bridge between pure awareness and the identified aspect of consciousness (mind). In other words, it is the pathway from movement to stillness.

The whole mind, as opposed to the fragmented mind, witnesses the totality of all functioning, or What-Is. In witnessing, the observer becomes the observed, the experiencer becomes the experiencing, or the seer becomes the scene. It is the breakdown of the subject-object relationship where the subject becomes the object, or vice versa.

In witnessing, things are simply seen for the way they are rather than the way they should or should not be. There is no "you" to filter or distort perception. The perceived "you" is also an object within the scene, among others.

So, things are seen, but there is no "seer". Therefore,

the witness is the "being" that remains in a natural state, silently watching all phenomena. It watches every feeling, thought, and sensation, but there is never a need to change or manipulate anything.

Witnessing brings about an acceptance of "What-Is", which is God's will. The acceptance is total, which even includes things that are unacceptable, like war, poverty, violence, racism, casteism, inequality, economic and environmental crisis, etc.

Acceptance, however, is not an attitude of resignation in the face of adversity. Therefore, I still condemn wars, racism, and violence, but with the renewed understanding that despite my best intentions and sincere efforts, things may or may not happen according to my desired outcomes. That even the above phenomena are expressions of wholeness.

The action that comes out of total acceptance has an entirely different quality to it. It is not driven by the individual's urge to assert his or her idea of righteousness. It comes from the recognition that all phenomena are happenings brought about by the Source, and not an individual's doing.

This recognition dissolves the burdens of shame, blame, guilt, pride, and arrogance. The whole mind sees the infinite intelligence beyond appearances. The limited fragmented mind, on the other hand, is a product of thinking. It believes itself to be separate from the whole mind. The fragmented mind is divergent and tied up with religion, region, culture, nationalism, profession, and other social identities.

The Notion of ME versus the Other

The divided mind creates the notion of "me" versus the "other." The other becomes suffering, irrespective of whether it is a friend, a relative, or a foe. We suffer our friendships and relationships more than our enemies. The fragmented mind lacks the strength to go beyond duality and tap into the infinite source of creativity and joy. It reminds trapped in identifications that propagate suffering in horizontal time.

The whole mind is a vertical thought. It is not characterized as a movement. It is the witness of the movement. The unchanging and eternal subject witnesses the changing objects. The fragmented mind keeps changing with identifications. It is the unreality born out of an inference brought about by ignorance. As a child, you never knew of yourself as the fragmented mind. At some point, it came about, through the identifications.

You were told that you exist independently of others. A newborn has no concept of separateness. It considers itself, the world, and the mother as one unit. Therefore, the newborn does not have a fragmented mind. But as the child grows into an adult, he or she undergoes worldly conditioning, which convinces them that they are separate from others.

This conditioning takes place in form of comparison and competition between siblings, friends, neighbors, work colleagues, and so on. Modern social media platforms are a breeding ground for separateness, where people posting selfies and giving intimate details about their personal lives crave attention, validation, and adulation. No matter how many likes or followers you have, nothing is ever enough.

Our suffering continues till we keep operating in the phenomenal world with a sense of separation.

The End of the Thinking Mind

Witnessing bring about an end to the thinking mind through the insight that it is a happening in the impersonal awareness of I AM. It is an impersonal phenomenon. The individual cannot cultivate the witness through any practice.

Witnessing happens spontaneously when the fragmented mind dissolves. The whole mind (witness) ceases the fragmentation, and what remains is the biological organism that acts spontaneously as and when a situation arises. Therefore, living becomes spontaneous and free from the burden of the thinking mind.

I remember, many years ago when I was troubled by afflicting thoughts, witnessing would begin spontaneously. A movement would start as a thought and expand horizontally as a chain, forming thinking where I would imagine the worst possible outcomes.

"If I fail my exam tomorrow, I won't get a good job; then my parents will abandon me, and my friends will think I'm a loser," and so on.

The end link of this chain of thoughts was either ending my life or harming myself in some way. Witnessing started cutting off this chain midway. The thought would arise, and at some point, there was this recognition that these are just thoughts. The chain would break abruptly and dissolves the whole toxic energy and negativity associated with thinking.

It restored the sense of calm that was disrupted by

thinking. It brought about the insight that there is no thinker. Now, without the thinker, the thoughts cannot continue for long. The discomfort gets cut off immediately.

Witness Consciousness Brings About Dispassion

As the thinking mind begins to dissolve, the grasping of identifications begins to loosen. Witnessing exposes all tricks of the ego-mind. One begins to see the divisive nature of thought and the futility of thinking. What emerges is the creative working mind that produces art of great magnificence. The working mind is never concerned with the outcome. It works in complete flow, contemplating the steps and strategies to execute a piece of work or art.

Vairagya, or dispassion with worldly things, comes about from witnessing.

In the Ashtavakra Gita, King Janaka asks Sage Ashtavakra, "What is the ultimate truth?"

The sage replies, "Know yourself as the pure consciousness, the unaffected witness of the phenomenal world, and you will know the truth."

However, note that dispassion cannot be cultivated by the individual through effort. Not by any suppression, repression, or denial. It comes from the impersonal understanding of the futile nature of thought. It comes with the understanding that the one creating desires in the hope of future fulfillment is an illusion. It comes with the understanding that clinging to either of the dualistic opposites of pain and pleasure perpetuates suffering. The understanding, in and of itself, brings relief, rather than doing something.

A couple of months ago, someone asked me how to be the witness. Look at the trap of the ego mind. It wants to be the witness because it has an agenda, that of self-expansion. Who wants to be the witness? The ego-mind thinks that by knowing the witness, it will become what it wants to be or unbecome what it is now. Whereas *now* is all there is. Now is the whole mind.

The misconception begins with a false assumption that I'm not the witness and that it is something to be acquired from the outside. You can never be the witness. How can you? You already are it. Your "being" itself is the witness. What creates separation is a belief that "I'm not it." That I must "do" something to get it.

Witness cannot be objectified because objectification required a subject or "you" to create an object. Any attempt to know the witness, through effort, creates a "you" that introduces separation. And as I mentioned in the beginning, witnessing is the breakdown of subject-object relationship.

Witnessing Brings About an Acceptance that Weakens the Ego

"One should remain as a witness to whatever happens, adopting the attitude, 'Let whatever strange things that happens happen, let us see!' This should be one's practice. Nothing happens by accident in the divine scheme of things."

Ramana Maharshi

Ramesh Balsekar emphasized that witnessing impersonally what happens, which means that we don't see events as a series of personal doings of individuals but act with the understanding that everything happens as per the cosmic law, brings freedom from shame, blame, malice, guilt, pride, arrogance, jealousy, resentment, and so on.

Acceptance is the complete understanding that no one is the doer of actions. Actions happen based on circumstances and the conditioning of the individual. It is only the mind that assigns a doer, either "me" or the "other," and labels the events as good or evil, moral or immoral, virtue or vice, and so on, which creates suffering as thinking in horizontal time. The conceptual thought "me," with its sense of personal doership, creates a story. And story creates conflicts in daily living, disrupting peace and harmony.

Witnessing is a watchfulness devoid of the subject or "me." It simply watches things and events without creating labels or judgements. In witnessing, there is no one to label or judge anything. And hence, there is no separation of consciousness from its content (thoughts, feelings, and sensations).

You can only be the witness; you cannot do witnessing as an activity because activity implies the subject. Witnessing does not happen in the domain of the analytical mind. It is beyond time. The analytical mind is a superimposition on the witness. The superimposed (fragmented) mind prevents us from realizing our natural state that is ever-present.

When the ego-mind realizes that its true nature is the witness and not the illusory thought of "me," it suspends all effort or personal doership. Therefore, the need to control and manipulate others for one's advantage begins dissolving. It is a recognition of the pure consciousness that powers all life.

Witnessing exposes the repeated thinking patterns of the ego-mind by bringing them to the light of pure awareness. The light destroys the darkness of unconsciousness. What remains is the peace that is our true nature. In that understanding, the problems of mundane living are no more seen as problems. In the absence of the thinking mind, life becomes spontaneous. And spontaneous living is peaceful living.

DO WE HAVE FREE WILL?

Do we have free will? Philosophers have been arguing and debating on this question for ages, but nothing concrete has come out. There are some who believe that we don't have free will, some others say that we have complete free will, and there are some who say that we have limited free will.

Instead of approaching this question of free will in an argumentative manner to justify my views, I'll make use of a concept and explore the question of free will on that basis. And as usual, you are always free to discard or accept the concept, based on your personal experience.

The concept can be summarized in the following few words: "You are not the doer of your actions; hence the sense of personal identification or agency is just an illusion."

How do you see yourself as an individual? The sense of personal identification arises because of the movement in consciousness, which we call the mind. The mind creates an illusion of the individual "doing" things. In deep sleep, there is no movement, and hence, the notion of "me" or ego or personal identification is missing. Only on waking up, do we say, "I slept".

Therefore, this personal identification with concepts, ideas, beliefs, dogmas, etc., becomes the source of never-ending suffering which we identify as the thinking mind. The thinking mind is the restless mind that either lingers in the dead past or in an imaginary future.

Simply put, you are not the individual that identifies with the thinking mind. You are the pure and eternal awareness in which the individual is simply an appearance.

Therefore, the mind-body complex is contracted energy or an instrument that simply functions according to the granted capabilities. In other words, the ego, or identification with name and form as a separate entity, is an illusion.

When there is no individual, where is the question of individual free will? The individual that appears to be doing things in the phenomenal world is an illusory projection on the screen of consciousness. You are the screen and not the character that is being projected.

But that said, you are to completely act as if you have complete free will because "you" or the created object cannot assume the will of the creator (or rather the projector) subject. In the movie called life, we are simply the created objects of characters (actors).

The only difference is that we don't know that we are in the movie, and we have no choice but to act our parts. The spiritual awakening happens when it is recognized that "we", per se, are not acting with our free will, but the action is happening through us according to the cosmic law.

We are the biological machines executing cosmic instructions. The script containing all possible actions and outcomes has already been written, where past, present, and future exist in superimposition, and we are merely acting our parts.

The suffering happens when the ego or the sense of personal identification, believing itself to be the "doer", thinks that it has the free will to change outcomes.

"There is neither creation nor destruction, neither destiny nor free will, neither path nor achievement. This is the final truth."

Ramana Maharshi

But I Do Have Some Volition to Make a Choice?

You may argue that in the larger context we don't have free will, but what about smaller scenarios? My assertion to that is that you do have the freedom to make a choice but what choice you make, and its outcome, is predetermined by the Universe. This is the part that majority of the people struggle with.

For example, you may assert that when I am offered a choice between two beverages, say tea and coffee, I have the volition to choose one over the other, don't I? And yes, at that time it may appear that you are choosing, but the choice has already been predetermined.

If you are aware at that moment, you'll notice that your choice, let's say coffee in this case, was the result of some internal or external process.

Maybe the presentation of the coffee was more appealing than the tea. Maybe the smell of coffee reminded you of a past pleasant experience of having a similar beverage somewhere else.

Maybe it was the positioning of coffee — say you're right-handed, and the coffee was placed on the right side, so it became your natural choice. Maybe you got up a bit fuzzy in the morning and you felt the need for a powerful stimulant.

There can be an endless number of causes that contribute to an action taking place. Whatever may be the cause, the choice and its corresponding outcome are predetermined. When your awareness is low, you will perceive this event as personal (I made the choice).

When you investigate deep, you'll notice that everything that happened had a precursor leading to that event. Therefore, randomness is as illusory as the existence of the individual making a choice.

What we perceive as randomness forms the basis of the cosmic law's execution. There are unknown variables that hide its cause. This idea is prevalent as super-determinism in Quantum theory. However, let's not go there, as scientific theories keep changing. Moreover, this idea is not likely to be accepted by the majority scientific community as it challenges the free will of the scientists to conduct experiments, and therefore, our trust in science as a whole.

However, I do not look at it that way.

Even if the scientists don't have complete free will to conduct experiments, it does not mean that science is wrong or that it cannot be trusted. The only thing is that the scientists cannot take complete credit for their findings, which may be a troubling idea for them to accept.

What you perceive as "your" choice is truly not yours. The outcome has been already decided and you are just a functioning instrument claiming the choice to be yours. This concept makes people uneasy, initially. It is true that it can be disturbing for most people.

We're so used to the idea of making things happen through our efforts and control. It is how the ego expands itself through doership. The ego believes itself to be the instrument of change. When things happen as expected, it creates pride and arrogance. And when they don't, it creates shame and guilt.

It continuously reinforces the sense of personal identification. Only when the ego gives up the sense of personal doership, which is also not in its control, does the surrender or liberation happen.

Liberation is simply the realization that you're not the doer of your actions, and that even others are not the doers of their actions.

In the words of Buddha, "Events happen, deeds are done, even the consequences happen, but there is no individual doer thereof."

Of course, you have the choice, but what is the quality of your choice or the option to exercise free will when every conscious or subconscious choice is determined by your past conditioning? Behind every choice that appears to be random is a subconscious process.

Even the desire to change the subconscious comes from the subconscious, which is again formed through conditioning. And the conditioning itself happens because of the Cosmic Law which lays out the destiny of every individual mind-body organism.

What We Misinterpret About Free Will?

Free will vs. Determinism has been a subject of an endless debate through times immemorial. Why? Because we live in duality. It is the nature of duality to exist with opposites. Therefore, if one side claims a certain view to be the truth, there will spontaneously be a counterview.

I believe my concept, particularly, is called "Hard Determinism" in Philosophy. Most people don't agree with the idea of not having free will because it attacks the ego and doership at its core.

Our society is immersed in doership from head to toe. The ego prefers concepts that strengthen it. Therefore, any idea that gives the impression of achievement or change in the world through personal effort is more appealing. It sees pride in its achievements.

In the event of failure, the ego loves to pin blame on others, play victim, complain, and whine about the situation rather than contemplate a constructive solution.

It's the ego's ploy to avoid facing the discomfort of shame that one carries within. Therefore, blaming and condemning becomes the default behavior.

But what happens when the ego suspends movement after the realization (impersonal) that it is not the doer and that everything happens according to the cosmic will?

Then one does not get involved in feelings of pride, arrogance, guilt, shame, malice, condemnation, jealousy, resentment, and more.

While the above feelings may surface temporarily,

their propensity to carry forward in horizontal time, as prolonged suffering, disappears.

Why do we struggle with shame? Because we believe to have the free will to "do" things. The realization of non-doership is a paradigm shift in one's perspective. It is liberation from the pain and suffering of guilt, shame, and resentment.

People spend their entire lives in resentment toward others, and the philosophical or psychological models do not help. Once you're free from the load of doership, which was brought about by the notion of free will, you remain peaceful, irrespective of the external circumstances.

You see the causal chain, but you don't fixate on a cause that leads to an event, and therefore, there is no complaining or whining, or other ill feelings towards anyone.

That's because you know the cosmic law is in execution and you are merely an instrument through which things appear to be happening.

The greatest misconception about determinism is the belief that since everything is predetermined, I must not do anything about a particular matter.

Is it even possible for you to not act? Or do nothing? If you can truly "do" nothing, you're already Zen. The action has to happen through the mind-body organism. Even when you don't make a choice it's a doing. You simply cannot "not" execute an action.

The psychophysical organism is designed by nature to execute actions. For example, if you say that I will not give an exam because the outcome is predetermined, it is your assumption that you know the cosmic law. It is doership under the pretext that "you know."

Whatever you do or don't do, the outcome is not in your control. But that should not be an excuse to not act or not decide. If you think you need to make a decision, do it. If you think you need to evaluate and then decide, do that.

"Whatever is destined not to happen will not happen, try as you may. Whatever is destined to happen will happen, do what you may to prevent it. This is certain. The best course, therefore, is to remain silent."

Ramana Maharshi

Why is the Idea of Not Having a Free Will Disturbing?

The basic problem with the idea of not having free will is that it challenges the very structure that forms the basis of society's functioning. When one does not have any free will, who is to decide what is right or wrong, good or evil, moral or immoral? These are the constructs on which modern society functions.

The contention is that the establishment or power structure that governs (or rather controls) society becomes powerless when it can't fix responsibility.

Let me address the bone of contention with the concept of not having free will, which is that it will give rise to a chaotic society where people will have no regard for laws and regulations.

Ramesh Balsekar would often say in his satsangs that even with the notion of having free will, chaos still exists in the world. Look around you and tell me one society, group, sect, country, or religion where there are no conflicts.

The law says that the person who commits a crime must receive punishment, but then if there's no free will, nobody commits a crime. Isn't it? So, do we need policing and law and order? We do. And here's why.

When a person commits a crime, let us say that a violent act takes place through a mind-body complex, nothing should stop society from taking action.

One can argue that he (or she) is not the doer of the act and that the action happened through him because of his past conditioning, which could be childhood abuse or adverse circumstances that propelled him to commit a crime.

My response to that is that if one is not the doer of his actions then one is also not the receiver of the consequences, but just like the violent act happened, a corresponding consequence will also happen as per the cosmic law.

The consequence may not be in accordance with our preferences. For example, despite compelling evidence, the perpetrator may go scot-free by exploiting loopholes in the law.

An innocent person may be punished for a crime that someone else committed. A criminal may receive a lighter sentence in comparison to the gravity of the crime he committed, or vice-versa.

Human intellect can never comprehend the magnitude of cosmic law because it is a product of cosmic law. For example, I can write a code to do some computation, but the code does not have the consciousness to know the purpose for which it was written.

The problem is that the ego-intellect thinks it knows

everything. Therefore, it claims to know everything or asserts that it will decode the cosmic law at some point in the future, through technology, or other means.

But again, I repeat Ramesh Balsekar's words that the created object cannot know the will of the creator Source.

Society not stopping the person from perpetuating a criminal act is assuming the cosmic law. How do you know you're not supposed to act and stop the crime? But know that despite your best intentions and efforts, you may not be successful.

If you say that since everything is predetermined, I should do nothing, that would again be an assumption of "I know". When in reality, since we cannot know the cosmic law, we must act from complete volition, knowing that the outcome is not in our control.

The judge, while awarding a sentence cannot assume the cosmic law (in the context of the argument) that we don't have free will. Even the judge's free will is shaped by his (or her) past conditioning, starting from childhood to the most recent experiences.

There is no absolute right or wrong here. The judge in the trial room must make a decision based on his present knowledge. If he starts doubting himself, he will not be able to decide.

Therefore, even the judge, as the acting individual, cannot be held responsible if the sentence he announces does not match society's expectations.

Whether his judgment will change the person or society, the judge can never know. Neither can he know if it's the right action or not. But he must act based on his understanding in the moment, without concerning himself with the outcome.

It is quite evident that very few prisoners get reformed in prisons. Many of them who go in for petty crimes actually become hardened criminals.

The reason is that the environment of prisons is often similar to the environment which shaped their brains to perform criminal activities. Even a home where parents lack empathy for their children can become a prison-like environment that can severely damage a child's psyche.

Another argument could be that we should show no compassion to people suffering because that's what is destined for them. It's their karma. Well, this is again the ego assuming the cosmic law. How do you know that that's what the Universe is asking of you?

If you're empathic and sensitive by nature, nothing should stop you from showing compassion to others. That's how the Universe designed you, so why not follow your instinct? Will you always be rewarded with love in return for your compassion? Absolutely not.

Some will respond to your compassionate nature, others won't; that's the design of life. You will learn about your natural inclinations and the path to follow through your own experience.

As I mentioned earlier, even with the idea that individual free will exists, chaos in the world will remain. Chaos and order are two sides of the same coin. One cannot exist without the other.

When people are held accountable (not shamed) and punished for their unkind actions, it does serve as a deterrent to some degree, and that is precisely why I advocate for stricter and more transparent law and policing, but I know that none of it will change fundamental human nature.

The change will happen only through the cosmic will which lays out the destiny of an individual mind-body organism.

The problem is that we cannot separate the action and the desired outcome. When you act in attachment to the desired outcome, two things are likely to happen:

1. When your action is successful it strengthens your sense of personal identification, "I am the doer," resulting in pride or arrogance.

2. When your action is unsuccessful it again strengthens the sense of personal identification by creating guilt or shame around failure. "I failed." "I could/should have done this/that."

The cosmic law does not consider your personal preferences while deciding the outcome of your actions. It does not give any preference to the individual's views because for it the individual does not exist.

My point is that the action must happen, but the consequences are not in anyone's control. You can't assume anything. All you can do is execute the action. And you can only do that when you remove your filtered perception.

The idea of individual free will gives hope to the ego that it can survive. That is why the ego loves to argue. The ego wants to remain relevant, so it does everything in its power to gain attention and validation, not knowing even that is part of the script and the outcome is already predetermined.

So, the ego questioning "doership" and free will also

happen according to the cosmic law. Your stumbling upon this message of non-doership was also predetermined.

This is something extremely difficult to absorb for the ego. The idea of not having personal volition or free will is extremely disturbing. And usually, it ends up in an inconclusive debate.

The ego loves to control and manipulate circumstances according to its preferences. That is fundamental to human nature. But this is precisely what causes suffering in life. That is why our society has so many conflicts at personal, religious, and economic levels.

With a firm idea of free will, the individual acts based on personal interests. The existence of the individual is by nature an alternating cycle of pain and pleasure, and suffering happens when the individual clings to either of the two.

The anticipation of pleasure in the form of materialism or even spiritual attainment brings pain and suffering.

No Free Will Is Not Fatalism or Nihilism

Many years ago, my family and I decided to buy a luxury vehicle. We used years of our savings into purchasing an expensive car (by Indian standards). However, the car dealer took the money but never delivered the vehicle. The money was substantial, and we were shocked and disappointed.

After a lot of bickering and unpleasant verbal exchange between me and the dealer, I decided to file a case of cheating against him. My lawyer was convinced that we had an upper-hand, and we would easily win the case.

The case continued for almost two years without any progress. The dealer was good at exploiting the loopholes in the slow Indian judicial system. He went absconding when the non-bailable warrant was issued against him. Somehow, he kept dodging and ducking, and nothing eventually happened.

Despite our best efforts, we never got our money back, and the dealer somehow continued to operate his business.

How do you look at this situation? The ego would look at the situation fatalistically, with a defeatist attitude.

At that time, my ego was hurt by the fact that I couldn't do anything. The thoughts in my mind were something on the lines of: "How did he fool me?" and "How could I make such a mistake?" and "I lost our family money because of my carelessness."

But then something miraculous happened which brought me great peace of mind. No, I did not get my money back.

I accepted what happened as the cosmic law. Is that fatalism or pessimism? Not at all. I relentlessly fought the case for two years. I did whatever I could do. I took the action that I thought was appropriate at the moment.

On accepting the cosmic law's outcome in this situation, my bitterness towards the dealer disappeared. I wish him well and think of him as my brother who needed something at that time, and it was my destiny to give him that.

From the egoic viewpoint, this may be seen as cheating, injustice, losing, or a quitter attitude, but for the Universe, this was simply an exchange between two objects.

The reason why concepts, theories, philosophies, beliefs, and ideologies fail to give us answers is that they're always formulated from a personal or individualistic point of view.

When the individual asserts his or her independent existence, he or she creates separation with the wholeness. The separation, by nature, is suffering.

In my situation with the dealer, I got to know that he was a repeat offender and had many lawsuits going against him. He was absconding most of the time and had spent some time behind bars. Who am I to judge or question the cosmic will?

Surrendering to cosmic will is most challenging for the ego. The ego-mind thrives by creating divisions such as good and evil, moral and immoral, justice and injustice, and so on.

I'm by no means implying that you give up on your identification of good and evil but remember that everything is relative. There are no absolute demarcations between good and bad that one can follow to live a peaceful life. All these concepts change with time.

In medieval times, challenging the Catholic concept of Geo-centrism (the Earth was the center of the universe, and all stars, planets, and the Moon revolved around it) was punishable by law. Galileo was accused of heresy for pursuing the helio-centric model.

The late medieval law punished abortion as a crime against unborn life. While abortion is widely accepted in the world today, there still are a few countries where it is considered illegal and punishable by law.

Just because things are relative in the phenomenal

world does not mean that we must cut off our identifications with everything. The idea of "not having free will" is not nihilistic. On the contrary, if understood in principle, it is liberating, for it says, "Let the Universe decide and I will simply execute the actions." It frees me from the load of responsibilities of doership.

When Buddha in his first noble truth said that the samsara (the world of names and forms) is dukkha (suffering, restlessness, and irritation), he did not mean it in the absolute sense. He gave the way out of dukkha by following a middle path which comprised of eight components.

Identifications, by themselves, are not evil or undesirable. They form the basis of inter-human interactions. Without identification, I wouldn't be able to write this essay, and you wouldn't be able to read it.

It is the grasping of identifications by the ego for creating strong beliefs and blindly following ideologies that causes suffering.

Freedom From the Bondage of Doership

It is difficult to know the nature of life as we know it, which is the basis for the cosmic law's functioning. We are the created objects that cannot know the "cosmic will".

Therefore, my concept is that when there's no "you," there's no question of "your" individual free will. But this is just my concept based on personal experience, and not "your" truth.

Whether this concept will or will not become "your" truth is the cosmic will and "your" destiny — the mind-body organism.

I'm not a religious man, but that is how I interpret the words in the Bible: "Father, if it's your will, take this cup of suffering away from me. However, not my will but your will must be done." – Luke 22:42.

However, this knowledge should not stop you from making choices. You are to operate in the world with a sense of free will knowing that the outcome is already predetermined.

There are things you'll do that will bring about a change that aligns with your preferences, but there'll be some doings that won't.

You are not to assume anything and work with your present thinking and knowledge to the best of your abilities. Again, it is not your action. The action happens through you.

The concept is that the individual must understand from personal experience the nature of his own illusory existence. And it is not merely an intellectual understanding but the awakening of the spiritual heart which brings about this shift.

This understanding offers tremendous relief from the burden of doership that we carry in daily living. Once the switch in perception happens, it significantly enhances our relationship with others. Not having free will is only troublesome for the ego with the sense of personal doership.

The ego likes to fix responsibility at a particular point in the chain of causation. What it fails to see is the whole picture. It's a defense mechanism of the ego to seek relief from its own fear and insecurity, but that never works.

The idea of teaching "them" a lesson to make

oneself feel better is pure doership. That's why the job of the judges is so challenging. They must keep aside their personal views and prejudices to serve the best interests of society.

They can't get swayed by emotions and must act in the most rational manner possible. That's why court trials take a long time, whereas the emotionally charged commoner complains about delays in the justice system. Imagine what would happen to our society if the judges behaved as people do on social media platforms.

Once the ego realizes (or the realization happens) that it is not the doer, there is no one to suffer. In my experience, this realization has been extremely liberating. It has sharpened my mind and fueled creativity in this mind-body organism.

You see, I'm not concerned with the outcome of my actions. I cannot concern myself with the thought that whether people will accept my ideas or not.

Freedom From Guilt & Shame

Say, if I react in the moment and hurt someone's feelings, nothing stops me from apologizing to that person with the sense that an unkind action happened through me. But at the same time, I don't beat up myself with guilt and shame for the way I acted, knowing that it was not my action.

Our triggers are not our creation, we get them through conditioning, so how can we be held responsible? If someone is a reactive or highly sensitive personality, it comes about as a result of parental, environmental, and societal conditioning.

So how can I alone be held responsible for an unkind act? But that said, this understanding does not relieve me from the consequences. When I hurt someone, I understand that that's what precisely had to happen. It was my destiny to create hurt and it was the receiver's destiny to feel hurt, and now it is my destiny to accept and face the consequences.

If I live with the guilt and shame for all my past unkind acts for the rest of my life, I will never be at peace. It's like living in Hell, for eternity. Only when I am free from guilt and shame, can I truly heal. And only when I heal, will I be able to love. People who carry hurt within are incapable of love.

Conclusion

There is usually a fear that the idea of no free will be misused by unscrupulous elements in society. And it will happen. Every teaching, concept, idea, or belief will always be misused and misinterpreted by some. People will use the concept to perpetrate violence and hostility.

They have done it using religion; they will do it using this concept. That is part of the functioning of totality. A knife can be used to either take a life or save a life. What happens is not an individual's choice but the functioning of cosmic law.

How and why? As created objects or biological machines, we will never know. And I'm okay with that, because I don't want to assume the subjectivity of the creator source.

I'm happy being the instrument through whom the cosmic energy expresses itself. I'm not even concerned about world peace, but it doesn't stop me from taking an action to express my ideas.

I may be the agent through which the message of non-doership is reaching you at this moment, but whether you awaken or not is not in my control.

Cessation of the obsessive thinking mind brings out the highest creativity, with genuine love and compassion for others. It can happen only when the ego realizes that it has no free will.

And that's because the individual realizes that behind all appearance is the same consciousness operating through all. We are one, and we are much more than this limited psychophysical organism we believe ourselves to be.

Although I assert that there is no free will, my goal is not to debate and prove this concept. If you think that you have complete free will to make a choice, go with that idea — maybe that's how the Universe wants you to explore life.

Our strong identification with the idea that "we know" becomes the cause of our greatest misery. The individual asserting its existence with complete free will takes on the load of doership and suffers.

I accept it is not easy to accept this idea. We are so conditioned to exercise control, and hence the idea that we're not in control, appears terrifying. We are so occupied with finding solutions to our problems that we completely ignore where the problems come from.

Ask yourself, "Am I at peace? Am I in harmony with existence?" Because all this discussion is meaningless if we're not at peace.

Peace of mind is not a goal for the individual to achieve. Peace or stillness or pure love is our true nature over which all perceivable objects in the form of ideas, thoughts, beliefs, dogmas, etc., are just super-impositions.

To be at peace, we need to understand our relationship with ourselves because that's what determines our relationship with others.

So, do we have free will? I'll say that we do, but the quality of that free will is predetermined. Is that an absolute fact? I don't know and neither do I recommend following any model to establish the truth. The truth must come from your personal experience.

ENLIGHTENMENT IS NOT AN EXPERIENCE

Any effort towards enlightenment or self-realization leads to the strengthening of personal identification. There's no individual person that ever gets enlightened. It is simply the end of "me and my story."

Ramana Maharshi was all about seeking the "Self". He relentlessly emphasized that "Self" is the highest truth. Nisargadatta Maharaj called it the "Supreme Reality", traditional non-duality teachers called it "Brahman", and the New Age spiritual teachers describe it as "Pure Consciousness", or pure awareness, wholeness, suchness, and more.

No matter what you call it, every attempt to describe it reduces it to a concept, and that's where the problem arises. The moment you try to explain the unexplainable, unimaginable, and indescribable, you reduce it to a state — as something desirable, and a worthy goal to attain.

The mind begins contemplating tricks and strategies to access a state of pure and permanent bliss where no suffering exists—a state of everlasting happiness and peace. There is no permanent state! How do you experience lasting happiness with an aging body that is decaying every minute? What do you do about the non-stop chattering mind?

Making the mind responsible for quieting the chattering mind is not a good idea. Ramesh Balsekar said that quieting of the chattering mind happens through the grace of God and not by the individual's effort. It is the mind that says, "I'm going to silence the mind through arduous practices and disciplines."

Investigate it and you'll see the paradox. The mind cannot solve this puzzle thought effort. Even the slightest effort in the direction of enlightenment is a diversion from one's true nature that is already enlightened.

Such an endeavor is guaranteed to fail. It's like employing a thief to protect your valuables or putting an arsonist in charge of the fire engines. The mind cannot annihilate itself through effort. Effort is an obstruction to self-realization— the realization that you already ARE what you seek. And what about the aging and ailing body? It's not in our control. Though we can make the body resilient with exercise, we can't prevent aging and death. Therefore, the illusory thought "me," that wants enlightenment, cannot get it, because the true enlightenment is its own absence.

"Enlightenment is total emptiness of mind. There is nothing you can do to get it. Any effort you make can only be an obstruction to it."

Ramesh Balsekar

When the mind realizes that it can't do anything about practically everything that happens in life, it comes up with the most cunning idea of enlightenment. It objectified the "Self" and makes it a personal quest to attain the permanent bliss of the "Self". Based on our idea about how an enlightened person should behave, we create an image and project it onto people.

The general conception is: "Enlightenment is going to do something for me; make me bigger, greater, and more worthy. People are going to address me as Guruji. I'll be the worshipful and most compassionate Guru. I will overcome all my addictions and bad habits. My relationships will become better. I will have more wealth, name, fame, and titles. And I will hold talks where I will enlighten others through mantra, tantra, Japa, and other means. I'm the chosen one."

Do you see what's happening? How the mind plays tricks? Relatively speaking, I have bad news and good news. The bad news is that the one who desires annihilation of ego is the ego, and the good news that *there is no ego.*

What Is Enlightenment Anyway?

I dislike the word enlightenment because when people ask about it, they have a particular perception or idea of what enlightenment should be. Does it mean that one has a flawless personality, is entirely in control of one's thinking, with the ability to manage emotions willfully?

Are they vegan? Do they care about animals? Are they into activism? Are they always politically correct? Do they talk about world peace and care for humanity? Do they ever get angry or upset with people? What should be their sexual preference? Do they do charity? And so on.

If you notice, the questions above are qualities that we like to see in the so-called enlightened masters. Therefore, we put them on a pedestal and project our desirable image onto them. We imagine near-perfect human beings that are infallible. The calm demeanor, along with the glittering robes and mala beads around the neck, gives the impeccable image of a perfect master.

Especially In India, a person wearing a robe, with a shaved head, and living life like an ascetic is worshipped by people as an avatar of God. The idea of renouncing the world for higher spiritual attainment — call it moksha, freedom, enlightenment, or whatever you like, is appealing to the common man. The message by the masters is, "Do as I tell you, and you will get it. I have the perfect recipe to enlighten you mere mortals. I have the mantra to give you immortality—freedom from the suffering of the endless cycles of birth and death."

To be honest, some of these are genuine masters with good intentions. For example, Nisargadatta Maharaj's Guru, Siddharameshwar Maharaj instructed him to stay with the "I-thought." Nisargadatta Maharaj earnestly followed his instruction and attained self-realization. Even Ramana Maharshi advocated self-inquiry to his disciples. The intention behind such instructions was not to make the "person" realized, but to enable their minds to discriminate the unreal from the real. Such masters do not come across as authority; as all-knowing. They are simple in their ways, and one feels peace in their presence. They do not rely solely on words to deliver the message. For the ripe minds, their presence is enough.

However, there are some people who proclaim themselves as the perfectly enlightened masters with the special power to awaken others. They spend decades studying scriptures like the Vedas and Upanishads. They flawlessly recite verses from the great scriptures with pride and enthusiasm. They claim that they are above all worldly desires, prescribe the same to others, but remain surrounded by wealth themselves. They claim to have something special that others don't have. They create non-profit organizations and run them like corporate businesses with complete political support.

And all this spiritual showmanship appeals to the ordinary people because most of them have a poor self-image. They project their own desirable traits onto these masters and create expectations. When the enlightened masters falter, these people are the first to push them from the pedestal.

There are countless cases of spiritual masters going rogue or engaging in unholy acts behind closed doors. It reminds me of a story that the Ramesh Balsekar told us in one of his satsangs.

There was a renowned spiritual guru in Mumbai who ran a popular foundation. Millions of people visited this guru to seek his blessing. A man was so influenced by the guru's teachings that he left his corporate job to join the foundation.

After the long day's discourse, the guru would retire into his room to rest. Only a handful of people were allowed in his room. As this man grew closer to the guru, he got the privilege of entering the guru's room in case of emergencies.

One day he wanted to discuss an urgent matter with

the guru, so he entered the room late in the evening. To his shock, he found the guru in a compromising situation with a young man. He froze for a while as he watched the scene and then quietly went out of the room, closing the door.

He felt disgusted and resigned from his position in the foundation the very next day. He was so upset that he did not even want to see the guru's face. However, at other people's insistence, he decided to meet the guru before leaving the foundation.

He and the guru sat face-to-face, and there was silence for some time. Then the guru persuaded him to stay, but he refused. The guru's final words to him were, "You have created the problem, and now you only have to solve it." After that, he left, never to come back again.

How would you analyze this situation? Was the guru at fault for hiding his affair with a young man and his sexual preference? Or were the people at fault for projecting an idealized image onto a man based on their conditioning — the things they perceived as holy and unholy? In Indian conservative culture, spiritual masters are often judged for their personal preferences and behaviors. When people dictate how an enlightened guru should behave, it becomes easy for unscrupulous elements to exploit their vulnerabilities.

In another anecdotal account by Jiddu Krishnamurti, he spoke about a young monk who came to see him. This young fellow in his early twenties got himself operated on through a medical procedure to get rid of his sexual desire.

Through years of conditioning by the religious authorities, he had started to believe that his liberation (another covert word for enlightenment) was marred by his inability to control his sexual urges. He was in tears when he met Krishnamurti but could do nothing as it was too late. If the idea of enlightenment is to deny worldly pleasures and subject oneself to torture through sexual restraint for one's entire life, then it is a twisted thought.

How can a saintly person have worldly material desires? You see, our body is also material, and it doesn't understand the concept of enlightenment as projected by our minds.

I'm not saying that every person in a robe is a rogue. I've met some genuine masters who I know have deep spiritual understanding. They don't claim they are enlightened or that enlightenment is theirs to give to the others. They don't prescribe hard discipline and give dogmas. They operate from a place of compassion and love, and not authority. They never claim to be infallible, nor do they put up an act. They remain authentically themselves. What I am saying is that we can't judge a master by his choices and personal preferences.

Deliverance of Spiritual Understanding

Spiritual awakening is not about achieving a permanently blissful state, but the breakdown of illusory structures of the ego-mind; the structures that identify with "I," "me," and "mine." Awakening tears into the link of interconnected opposites and reveals the futility of the thinking mind. It is the impersonal and instantaneous recognition of the truth that there is no permanent state in duality, and that the subject-object split is an illusion.

For most people, spiritual awakening is a brutal revelation because the ego, after having a glimpse into its non-existence, becomes restlessness initially. In some cases, this insight causes deep existential crisis and depression. Personal enlightenment, on the other hand, is a delusion, where the individual imagines living in a permanent state of ecstasy.

While spiritual awakening happens instantaneously, the deliverance happens gradually. Deliverance is the complete embodiment of the concept that there is no individual that does any action through personal volition.

While awakening is beyond time and space, deliverance operates in duality, within time. As this understanding of the above concept deepens, the mind settles down, realizing its illusory existence. When the understanding dawns that everything happens according to the cosmic law, the relationship conflicts begin to dissolve.

Just as we accept ourselves, we also accept others as not the doers. The depths to which this deliverance penetrates the individual's mind is God's will, and the destiny of the individual mind-body organism.

In a nutshell, the following quote from Ramesh Balsekar explains it all. "In the words of Buddha, actions happen, deeds happen, and even the consequences happen, but there is no individual doer thereof."

Even after final deliverance, the conflicts may still arise in the moment, but nothing gets propagated in horizontal time as suffering. So, a hurt in the moment, does not become resentment in horizontal time. The emotions may still arise in the moment, as no one can control what happens in the moment, but nothing becomes suffering in time. In other words, living becomes spontaneous.

"The happiness you are seeking is not to be found in the flow of life, but in your attitude toward whatever

life brings."

Ramesh S. Balsekar

As this understanding deepens, the dispassion towards the materialistic life occurs naturally as the individual is no more concerned with the results of their actions. The ego, realizing that only the cosmic law prevails, suspends the sense of doership, resulting in peace, tranquility, and compassion. The striving for personal excellence and growth transforms into service for others. It is no more about "me."

A gratitude arises towards the awareness, for granting this life experience. There is an unconditional acceptance of "What-Is". Such an acceptance is surrender to God's Will, where the God is not a separate all-powerful entity in manifestation, but the totality of all functioning or the pure consciousness; the choiceless awareness that is the witness of all phenomenality.

The individual continues to live life as before, but there's a shift in one's perception towards life. The shift is that the involvement in worldly affairs dissolves. The self-realized individual, the one that has recognized its illusory nature, or *jivanmukta,* does not deny anything in the world, but at the same time, he does not get too attached or involved. He still engages with the world in a meaningful way, but there is no involvement in the form of desire to change the world according to personal preferences.

Before spiritual awakening, the individual with the sense of personal volition becomes attached to doership. He puts effort to achieve his desires, which strengthens his sense of personal identification. He works hard to attain high status, wealth, and fame. He derives his sense of self-worth by the value of things he accumulates; by the brand of clothes, by his collection of shoes and watches, by the latest smartphone that he holds, and so on. For him, things like money, power, position, stature, and prestige matter more than peace of mind.

He believes that he's a separate individual living in separation from the rest and must prove his worthiness to gain other people's validation and acceptance. Therefore, the idea of achieving wealth and fame through hard work appeals to him.

But the problem is that it further increases the separation, which itself becomes the cause of suffering. I'm not judging anyone because I recognize that even running after fleeting pleasures happens as per God's will. We can't blame an individual for his choices and behaviors because he didn't choose anything. The individuals are products of their genes and conditioning, which was never in their control. So, the idea is not to condemn people for their choices but to point out the unconsciousness, that blinds the ego, leading to suffering.

Even a sage, with complete deliverance, may choose to live a luxurious lifestyle, but his (or her) choice do not define him. He does not derive a sense of self from the items he owns. He is perfectly okay even if everything is taken away from him in an instant. He does not demand anything. He does not reject anything. As I mentioned earlier, he lives spontaneously with the understanding the only God's Will prevails.

In a society deeply entrenched in consumerism, it is commonly seen that most people are always on a chase to better themselves by acquiring external possessions, something to make them feel whole. Self-realization is the recognition that wholeness is one's true nature and that the separation is an illusion.

Make no mistake, this can happen even in spiritualism. It is called spiritual materialism. Some time ago, a girl approached me with kundalini-related questions. She was experiencing a surge in kundalini energy, so much so that she could not focus on work or family.

As a result, her life was in disarray. She desperately wanted a solution to her Kundalini awakening problem as it was causing discomfort and panic. She was not happy when I suggested that she speak to a counselor or a therapist. The psychological picture of Kundalini rising was so firmly embedded in her mind that she didn't want to explore an alternative approach.

She wanted instant liberation from pain and suffering. When she approached, she projected an image of a guru onto me. As I did not provide the solution she hoped for, she immediately pushed me off the pedestal, and I never heard from her again.

Most people have preconceived notions about spirituality and enlightenment, and it is incredibly challenging to break down these fictitious ego structures. They believe that through enlightenment, they will achieve something that will somehow make them better than the rest. And hence, enlightenment becomes another desirable object to attain, just like the other material desires.

Enlightenment does not offer a solution to any problem. It is the understanding that the problems created by the thinking ego-mind have no answers in the outside world. That the root of all question is itself a piece of fiction. The search for personal enlightenment is a ploy to avoid the discomfort of facing ourselves to see who we are. Enlightenment is not an experience but the recognition of the infinite "being", which is the ground of all experiential awareness.

The ego-mind identified with a blissful experience, or a vague idea of it, keeps chasing it for the rest of its life. You may see Buddha, Jesus, and Krishna in mediation, but they will all go away eventually. All images fade but the presence where images appear remains ever-present.

After a spiritual awakening, the individual directly sees the illusory nature of the world. All ideas, beliefs, and concepts lose their grip on him. He no longer chases ideas to enhance his personal sense of self.

He clearly sees the futility of the obsessive thinking mind and how it leads to unnecessary involvement that causes pain and suffering. It is the dawn of something beautiful — witnessing. In witnessing, things and events are seen for what they are, and not from the biased perspective of the ego-mind.

But what about paying bills, mortgage, student loans, work deadlines, and relationships? All of these remain, but the involvement of ego in the drama disappears. A self-realized person continues to work and pay bills, but there's a greater realization in the background of awareness that all of life is illusory and one is already what they seek. When the load of doership is gone, peace is the natural outcome.

There's No "You" That Ever Gets Enlightened

There's a misconception that it's the individual entity or person that gets enlightened through effort. The notion of the personal self, in and of itself, is the cause of pain and suffering.

That's why all great masters say that enlightenment happens when the spiritual seeker stops seeking. As long as the seeking goes on, the personal self, or "me", deludes itself, thinking that it can become something more by attaining something that it perceives of higher value.

The seeking itself becomes the cause of suffering as it enhances the sense of personal identification or the ego. I can realize the self if I meditate for fifteen hours every day. I can do it by reading books and scriptures. I can do it by dedicating my life to a spiritual master. I can do it by renouncing the world.

You see, this "I" thought itself is the source of all problems. It attaches itself to thoughts, ideas, and beliefs, whereas liberation from suffering lies in the dissolution of this very thought.

Therefore, any effort towards self-realization will lead to the strengthening of personal identification. Ramana Maharshi said that self-realization is the simplest thing. There's no YOU that gets enlightened. It is simply the end of "me and my story."

The mind creates the notion of "me" that struggles in the world to achieve greatness. And in that endeavor, it goes through the hardships and trials and tribulations of life.

The story includes success and failures. The "me" takes pride in success and achievements and feels guilt and shame in failures. Both pride and shame perpetuate the personal self. Pride leads to arrogance. Guilt and shame lead to dejection. It's a never-ending cycle of pain and suffering.

Gautama Buddha practiced asceticism through hard

concentration and austerities for six years. He tortured himself by eating less to such an extent that his ribs had started showing.

In this ordeal, he gained five companions who practiced rigid discipline alongside. In the end, Buddha realized the futility of such practices and chose to adopt a middle path of moderation.

Seeing this, his companions left him as they felt he had diverted from the original path. It is the way a common man views the world. When the sense of doership is strong, we think that everything must come through hard work. We feel that enlightenment is an achievement that must be gained through effort. That is okay for worldly pursuits, but for self-realization, the effort must drop. The effort implies silence of the mind.

The word self-realization is a bit of a misnomer because it implies there's a separate entity that has to realize something that is apart from it. The problem is that we're using language to communicate the incommunicable.

The language in and of itself is dualistic, and hence, it's impossible to describe what wholeness means, using language. Even the word non-duality is merely a concept, a feeble attempt to explain that which cannot be explained. There's no such thing as a non-dualist practicing non-dualism.

It's absurd to see that some modern-day teachers argue about the teachings of Traditional Advaita and Neo-Advaita. They are all concepts. Self-realization is not an intellectual endeavor.

As Ramana Maharshi called it, the "Self" cannot be realized by the intellect because it's not a product of the illusory mind but the supreme consciousness that illuminates the mind and the world of name and forms.

The intellect at some point gives up after wrestling with thoughts, ideas, and beliefs. When everything fails, the mind settles down. It is then that the Heart awakens, and one feels at home. In reality, you were always home.

"Having never left the house, you are looking for the way home."

Nisargadatta Maharaj

The Heart is the place of deep silence that dissolves the contracted energy called "me" back into the boundless energy or source. The Heart is the eternal "Self".

Therefore, you can't learn by reading a thousand books what a glimpse of silence can teach — the highest knowing that behind the world of appearances, which is seen as multiplicity of names and forms, there's ONE consciousness that pervades everything.

The world exists in consciousness. It disappears when you're asleep. But the "Self" is the eternal constant that underlies all states: waking, dreaming, and deep sleep.

In the end, peace of mind in daily living is what matters rather than some abstract idea of enlightenment. A peace that remains unaffected by worldly events and enables us to be in our natural state of serenity and tranquility. I'm not the least concerned about "your" enlightenment. What I have for you is Nothing.

That is all what I have to say!

ABOUT THE AUTHOR

Jagjot is an Indian-born spiritual author and speaker who talks about Non-Duality or Advaita. He adopts a practical approach to non-duality rather than following fixed traditional systems and religious dogmas.

Jagjot believes that spiritual awakening has to be verified through direct personal experience, and the ultimate objective, so as to speak, is to cultivate peace of mind and daily living.

After relentlessly chasing material success for fifteen years in the corporate software industry, Jagjot felt tired and broken. Despite a well-paying job, he was depressed and lonely. Though he was doing well in his career, there was no sense of fulfillment or joy. The happiness and glory of a booming IT industry were nowhere to be found.

It was then that he decided to leave his corporate job and explore the spiritual path. And after a few years of seeking, he discovered something incredible. His spiritual awakening was sudden and intense, and he realized that what he sought was never apart from him.

He learned that all this time he was living in an illusion of separation, which was the cause of his pain and suffering. When the illusion disappeared, the Wholeness revealed itself, and it broke the last remains of what was perceived as the "me" in Jagjot.

After the awakening, Jagjot read the teachings of spiritual masters like Ramana Maharshi, Nisargadatta Maharaj, Jiddu Krishnamurti, and Ramesh Balsekar. The teachings of these great masters helped in deepening his understanding of the ONE non-dual truth.

Jagjot does not consider himself to be a spiritual teacher, Guru, or healer. He is simply a pointer in consciousness that seeks solace in delivering the message of peace and harmony in daily living.

His only objective is to help others discover the same peace or awareness he experienced. He has hundreds of articles on non-duality on his website jagjotsingh.com, videos on his YouTube channel, and podcast episodes on all major platforms.

Jagjot is freely available to anyone who wishes to discuss any spiritual matter. You can easily contact him, without hesitation, by visiting his website's contact page.

You can directly reach out to Jagjot via email: info@jagjotsingh.com

Other Title by Jagjot

I HOPE YOU
GET

NOTHING

OUT OF THIS

*Dialogues on Non-Duality
(Advaita)*

JAGJOT SINGH

Made in the USA
Monee, IL
18 February 2024

53731020R00098